Hyuepingka
0.0°C
5 0 Rad
0 0 Tox
bhngozanq-Upans
Traintruction
6,016ks
205u
utorisc S78
Photon Cannon

LIMITLESS SKY

NO MAN'S SKY® UNOFFICIAL DISCOVERY GUIDE

JEFF CORK

TRIUMPH
BOOKS

This book is book is available in quantity at special discounts for your group or organization. For further information, contact:

Triumph Books LLC
814 North Franklin Street
Chicago, Illinois 60610
Phone: (312) 337-0747
www.triumphbooks.com

Printed in U.S.A.
ISBN: 978-1-62937-327-0

Interior design by Patricia Frey
Cover design by Preston Pisellini

CONTENTS

Introduction .6

The Origins of No Man's Sky 8

Procedural Generation 14

Getting Started 22

Going Offworld. 46

Your Suit 60

Your Multi-Tool 66

Your Ship. 70

Exploring the World Around You 84

The Elements 98

Intelligent Life 106

Journey to the Stars. 110

Other Game Recommendations . . . 122

39u

Aik Hachib

INTRODUCTION

Welcome, traveler. You're about to embark on a journey unlike any other.

Ahead, you'll find planets to discover and explore, teeming with life and artifacts from those who have come before you. You could spend years fully charting a planet's surface, naming your discoveries for those who come after you, and mining the world for valuable resources.

But that's just the beginning.

Hop into your spacecraft and you can soar beyond the stars, setting a course for the complete unknown as you inch your way toward the center of the galaxy. How long that journey takes is completely up to you. Between you and that goal are quadrillions of unique planets, loaded with unpredictable creatures and breathtaking vistas.

Fully discovering everything there is to see in No Man's Sky is an impossible task, even if you tap into the collective hive-mind of every player who experiences this incredibly ambitious game. This guide won't even attempt to fully chart one of the game's 18 quintillion planets. Instead, it will provide you with everything you need to know to embark on your own unique journey.

Do you plan on living your virtual life as a peaceful explorer, leaving minimal footprints on each planet you visit while adding to the collective knowledge base? Would you rather find your fortune (and infamy) blasting apart trade vessels and avoiding the authorities as a space pirate? Or perhaps you'd like to learn the secrets of the universe by cooperating with alien cultures?

No Man's Sky can be overwhelming by design, but don't let its scale paralyze you. Regardless of how you choose to play, we'll give you the foundation you need to tackle the universe on your own terms.

Whether you're looking for guidance on what minerals and resources are worth your time, how to upgrade your weapons to meet their planet-carving potential, or how to get your hands on a ship that will become the stuff of legend, we're here to help.

No Man's Sky will surely be changing over the coming months and years as development continues and updates are released, but let's get started. We've got a lot of ground to cover, after all.

Note: *No Man's Sky is available on the PlayStation 4 and PC, and the two versions are functionally identical. For the sake of this guide, we'll be referring to the PS4 control scheme. The button mapping will be different on PC, but the references to gameplay and the overall flow are the same on both platforms.*

THE ORIGINS OF NO MAN'S SKY

Looking at No Man's Sky, it's easy to assume that it's the creation of a massive team of developers, from a studio with a track record of producing massive open-world games. The reality is much different—and far more interesting.

Before it wowed the world with the prospect of discovering an entirely new universe, Hello Games found success in a charming little game about a motorcycle stuntman.

Hello Games was founded in 2009 in Guildford, England. The town, located a quick train ride away from London, is a hotbed of English game development; it has served as home to game studios that have created top-tier titles such as Burnout, LittleBigPlanet, Fable, and many others. After working at a variety of Guildford studios, four developers—Ryan Doyle, Grant Duncan, Sean Murray, and Dave Ream—decided to break away from larger companies and form their own indie studio.

That studio became Hello Games, and its first title was the PlayStation 3 game Joe Danger. The side-scrolling action game, released in the summer of 2010, featured the titular stuntman in a series of escalating feats of derring-do. Players had to time their motorcycle's jumps and calculate their landings to score big—and avoid getting scorched by fiery hoops, devoured by ravenous sharks, or other career-ending failures.

The game was a success, and the small team worked on bringing it to the Xbox 360. They also hired a few more employees and began work on its sequel, Joe Danger 2: The Movie. The follow-up added more variety to the formula, giving Joe more vehicles to choose from and dropping him into a variety of different movie-style action sequences.

Audiences seemed to like Joe Danger and what Hello Games was doing, but Murray, programmer and studio co-founder, was growing restless. He had what he later described as a bit of a breakdown, and worried that the new studio, which he and his friends had founded to express their own creativity, was heading down an all-too familiar path. After Joe Danger 2, what would come next? Joe Danger 3? Joe Danger 4? As much as he loved the little guy, it wasn't a future he was thrilled about.

Murray set up a private office within the studio, and for a year worked on a secret project once his work on Joe Danger 2 was finished. He created another new game engine, but this was far more advanced than the one he had worked on with Joe Danger. Joe Danger gave players the thrill of being a stuntman. This new project would possibly give players an entire universe.

Eventually, Murray took Duncan and Doyle aside and explained what he was working on. Until then, it had been clouded in mystery. For years, Murray had been fascinated with games such as Elite, which let players explore space and forge their own paths.

He'd wanted to be an astronaut for a time, and games turned out to be the next best thing. What if he could live that childhood fantasy through his own creation?

The three of them expanded work on the project, which was called Project Skyscraper. Hello Games is a small studio, but that core team wanted to work on this exciting new game in isolation. They took what seems like an extreme measure and set up a studio within the studio—complete with its own locks and entrance. They decorated this new space with covers of old sci-fi paperbacks, filled with fantastical visions of far-flung planets and alien ships. These would provide inspiration while the team worked on what would become No Man's Sky.

Murray says that it's easy to see their isolation as an act of selfishness—especially when the rest of the team was so desperate to learn what their co-workers were toiling away on—but that it was ultimately one of generosity. The people at Hello Games are more than co-workers; they're friends. Even now that the team has grown to just over a dozen or so people, it's a tight-knit group. Murray wanted the game to be more than just a kernel of an idea before he shared it with them. He wanted to impress them with a clear vision for what, exactly, they'd been working on all this time.

That moment came in 2013, when the studio was given the chance to debut the game at the VGX 2013 game awards. It was a big opportunity, guaranteed to give the fledgling game plenty of attention from gamers and the games press. Murray and his team agreed, and then it was time for them to show the rest of the group at Hello Games what they'd been working on in secrecy for several years.

The response was one of awe, as they were shown the trailer for the game, and got presentations on the game itself and its various components. Yes, you could fly off a planet's surface in your spaceship. No, there wouldn't be any visible load times. Yes, the galaxy is that big. The rest of the team, which had been working on the iOS game Joe Danger Touch, couldn't wait to dig into this exciting new game.

The trailer made a big impression on the rest of the world, too. At first, few believed that such a game would even be possible, let alone possible from such a small team. Over the course of several showings in the following years, including stage presentations at E3 and guest appearances on talk shows like *The Late Show with Stephen Colbert*, people began to believe.

The road hasn't been smooth, but it's led us to where we are now. The game was delayed several times, the final time only a month before its planned June 2016 release date. "Making this game is the hardest thing I've ever done in my life, but we are so close now, and we're prepared to make the tough choices to get it right," Murray explained on a blog post. "This is the hardest working, most talented team I've ever worked with, and I'm so proud of what we're doing. For all our sakes though, we get one shot to make this game and we can't mess it up."

And here we are. The game is out, and people are finally able to see just what this tiny team has cooked up. The amount of hype that had built up before its release was a mixed blessing, and the end result certainly isn't for everyone. But players who enjoy experiencing amazing new places and braving perilous conditions while exploring are likely to find dozens—if not hundreds or more—of satisfaction-filled hours.

No Man's Sky Discovery Guide

PROCEDURAL GENERATION

No Man's Sky features a vast galaxy, filled with more planets than you could hope to explore in a thousand lifetimes. Once that's settled in, you might find yourself asking, "OK, then how the heck did Hello Games create all of those planets? Are they secretly time-traveling immortals?"

While the developers are certainly talented, they don't have any kind of magical or godlike abilities. What they do have is a firm grasp of a technique called procedural generation.

We won't get too deep into the weeds here, but it's important to have a basic understanding of what that means. It will give you a greater appreciation for how everything fits together—from the virtual ground you're standing on, to the creatures you meet and the music that fills your ears. Without procedural generation, none of this would be possible, or at least not in the scale that we're able to experience.

First, let's think about traditional 3D game design. Everything you see is the work of talented artists, programmers, and designers. They create your characters, the tools and weapons that those characters use, and the worlds that you explore. In the vast majority of cases, developers are essentially working with virtual Lego bricks. For example, let's think about a game that features a house. That house has walls that make up an exterior, as well as interior walls that create rooms. Inside of those rooms are various bits of furniture, appliances, and other things that you'd expect to find in, well, a house.

Artists and 3D modelers don't create that house in one big block. Instead, for efficiency's sake, they break it up into smaller components. That way, they can reuse elements instead of having to remake them from scratch. A door that's used in one bedroom can be used in another. A dining-room chair can be duplicated to make a set. It saves time, particularly in a game that features multiple houses. Play enough games, and you'll notice that certain objects pop up several times, such as vending machines or garbage cans.

Most of the time, when level designers are creating spaces for the player, they'll manually place the

objects that the artists have created. In our house example, they wouldn't drop all of the decorations in a pile in one room and call it a day. Instead, they'll put things where players are expecting them—although in some game genres, like horror, the point is to surprise players with the unexpected. Regardless, people are setting the stage.

That handcrafted approach can lead to spectacular results, such as the incredibly detailed levels in the Uncharted series, the precise recreations of real-world tracks in the Forza Motorsports games, or even the tile-based worlds from older titles such as Super Mario Bros. When game worlds get extremely large, however, you have a couple of options. You can hire an extremely large team of developers, but that's (appropriately enough) extremely expensive. The other option is to rely on procedural generation.

Procedurally generated games still rely on the same basic building blocks that traditional games use, though they're used differently. Rather than having a person or team of designers manually placing objects in the world, procedurally generated games let computers do much of the heavy lifting. Games have been using this technique for decades. In Rogue, for instance, players could brave a new danger-filled dungeon every time they played. More recently, Minecraft generates vast new spaces for players to explore at the press of a few buttons.

Developers don't drop all the virtual chairs, tables, and walls into a folder and expect the computer to magically build a house, however.

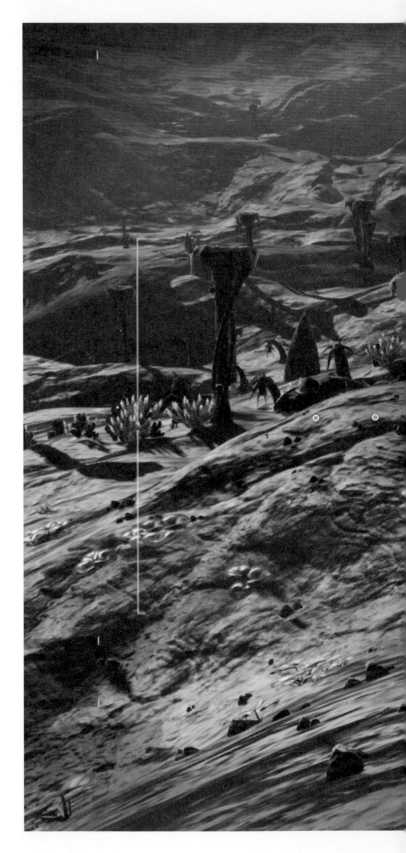

First, programmers have to create rules and guidelines for what's expected in a house. Houses usually have a minimum of four exterior walls. Doors lead to other rooms, and if they lead to the outside on a second story, there had better be an attached deck or set of stairs. Toilets should go in bathrooms, not lined up against the kitchen table. Once all the rules are established, the computer can create an entire housing development filled with slightly different houses that still function as houses.

In the case of No Man's Sky, Hello Games developed complicated computer algorithms that govern virtually every element of the game. When you start the game, it's almost certain that you're going to begin on a planet that nobody from that team has seen, with creatures that none of them are familiar with, in a solar system that's as much of a mystery to its creators as it is to you. But because of the work that the developers have put in over the course of several years, they're confident that it will be an interesting and satisfying place to explore.

When games are procedurally generated, most of the time it's limited to the layout of an environment or the placement of objects, such as trees and rocks, within those environments. With No Man's Sky, however, it runs much deeper. The creatures that you see are also procedurally generated—including the way they move and sound. Artists at Hello Games created hundreds of different creature parts, like head shapes, limbs, tails, horns, and other parts drawn from real-world animals. The computer assembles those various bits into fully realized alien life,

finishing them off with a vast array of different types of fur, scales, skin, colorization, and other visual flourishes.

From there, the system can determine how the newly formed creature flies, walks, slithers, or swims, depending on the position of each limb, the size of the finished creature, and other factors. So a small horselike beast might gallop as expected, but something that looks like a gargantuan scaled goat might stomp around a valley. Something with wings might fly, unless its mass is too large to prevent that from happening.

On the audio side, creature vocalizations are generated based on the general acoustics of their body, head, and nose shapes. It's all accompanied by a soundtrack that's—you guessed it—procedurally generated based on tiny audio pieces created by the band 65daysofstatic.

Thanks to all those elements, Hello Games (and its complicated tech) has created a magnificent universe for players to explore for decades to come. And with that, it's about time we get started.

smodum Ozdok
5°C   1.1 Rad
        11. Tox

GETTING STARTED

You'll likely feel a kinship with your character during the opening moments of No Man's Sky. When you awaken on the planetary system, it's clear that you've suffered some kind of crash landing and you're a little dazed from the collision. Thanks to the magic of procedural generation, the specifics of your starting scenario are going to be different from anyone else's, but there are some critical overarching elements to cover before we disembark.

In the first few moments, your suit's various systems go online in an automated diagnostics routine. One by one, the elements of your heads-up display, or HUD, flicker onto the screen. Before we dive into the game itself, let's take a moment to acclimate ourselves to what exactly we're looking at.

On the lower-left portion of the screen, you'll get information that's vital to your survival. At the top of that section, you'll see the levels of your suit's life-support and environmental-support systems in

Gelsehan GZ585

36.6°C | 0.0 Rad
2.6 Tox

Gelsehan GZ585

36.6°C | 0.0 Rad
2.6 Tox

Gelsehan GZ585

36.6°C | 0.0 Rad
2.6 Tox

a meter. Below that, you'll see the name of the planet that you're on. Rounding out that corner is the temperature, in Celsius, as well as the current levels of radiation and environmental toxicity. You may find yourself on an oppressively hot planet, with scorching temperatures that are incompatible with native life. Or you could be lucky enough to find yourself on a temperate paradise. Regardless, this section of the HUD is a quick reference to see how you're faring against the world itself.

Above that, on the upper left, are the portions of the HUD devoted to you, the meaty little thing inside the suit. The meter reflects the strength of your shield, which is the barrier protecting you from taking physical damage. Once the automated life-support systems fail, your shield is depleted. Or your shield can be depleted from falling from unsafe heights or from encounters with dangerous animals. Once it's gone, the health pips, represented by the boxes with crosses on them, will tick away. Once they're gone, you're dead. Don't worry if that happens, though; you can visit your "grave" where you expired, and reclaim your lost inventory.

In the middle center is a simple waypoint display. It's a particularly helpful tool for finding your ship. If you do find yourself lost, simply spin in a circle until you see your ship's icon, turn until it's in the center, and start walking in that direction.

On the upper right are the portions devoted to your multi-tool. Your multi-tool is a handy device that's one part weapon, one part mining tool, and one part scanner. It's an essential piece of equipment, and you can see what mode it's in—between the mining beam and the boltcaster, which you don't have yet—as well as a meter that shows the heat levels of the mining beam when it's being used. You can also check out the tool's remaining fuel. That row of five icons to the left of the percentage shows the amount of Sentinel attention you've gathered at the moment. As they fill, the greater the threat. We'll get back to that in a minute.

Finally, you can see your objectives on the bottom right. As we begin, you have several tasks to worry about. But first, let's take a look at the area that's immediately around us.

There are plenty of interesting things to check out in the nearby debris field, not the least of which is your smoldering ship. You can walk up to its cockpit and enter the crashed vessel, but it won't start—its pulse engine and launch thrusters were damaged, and it's up to you to make repairs.

There's actually a fair amount of damage to repair, some of which is extended to your multi-tool. If you try to scan the environment by pressing L3 on your gamepad or pull up your analysis visor with L2, you'll get notifications that both of the devices are offline. You'll need to collect 25 carbon and 25 iron to make those repairs, respectively. Take a look at the area around the ship, and you'll see several crates and other containers. Hold down the square button to interact with them, and you can see and take their contents. Some of the smaller containers may contain the required elements that you're looking for. If not, don't worry.

One of the items around your ship is very important: a distress beacon. Interacting with that and choosing to follow the path that follows sets the game's story mode in motion. No Man's Sky

Gelsehan GZ585

36.6°C | 0.0 Rad
2.6 Tox

Traintruction

Units: 0 ⊕

STARSHIP INVENTORY (15 SLOTS)

Ⓐ EXOSUIT | STARSHIP | MULTI-TOOL Ⓓ

Rasamama S36
Install technology and manage your starship's cargo

WEAPONS

HEALTH

SCAN

HYPERDRIVE

RETURN Ⓟ

Iron // Oxide
Destroy

Gelsehan GZ585
36.6°C | 0.0 Rad
2.6 Tox

is an exploration game, but choosing to follow the Atlas is a great way to get your feet beneath you as you play the game. It provides some structure to the opening hours, too, and it's highly recommended that you follow its path. For the purposes of our overall walkthrough, we'll assume that you're doing just that. But first, of course, we need to get off our starting planet. Back to the repairs.

The launch-thruster repairs require several carite sheets, which are an item that you can craft yourself after collecting enough iron, as well as plutonium to fuel the thrusters and get off the ground. For

the pulse engine, you'll need to track down 200 heridium, 20 zinc, and two additional carite sheets. Each carite sheet is built using 50 iron. Let's get the goods.

Your multi-tool's mining beam is a slick bit of tech, reducing plants, rocks, and animals to their elemental essence. Fortunately for us, the elements that we're looking for are in relative abundance across the galaxy—you just need to know what to look for. Carbon can be found from plants and animals. Iron is typically found from rocks. Zinc can be found by interacting with yellow flowers.

Plutonium is found in spiky red crystals. Finally, heridium is hard to miss—it's typically concentrated in towering rectangular deposits.

To mine, walk near the object that you want to dissolve into piles of elements, and hold down the gamepad's right trigger. A beam should emit from your multi-tool, and rocky chunks should be sucked up into your device. Keep an eye on the overheat meter, since it has a tendency to fill up quickly when you're starting out. You can upgrade the beam to mine more efficiently later, but for the time being just make sure it doesn't turn red. There's no real penalty if it does, aside from wasted time. You can mine continuously if you release the trigger

for about a second when it's close to overheating and then resume. That short window of inactivity is enough to keep the multi-tool working efficiently.

Have you seen those little drone-like orbs floating around? Those are Sentinels. They're essentially intergalactic watchmen, and they can be a pain or barely noticeable—again, it's the luck of the draw. They're typically attracted to the sounds of mining or of animals dying, so keep that in mind when you're grabbing resources. If they do fly up to you, you may want to stop mining and wait for them to go away. Otherwise, you'll probably end up in a scrap, which isn't advised at this point in the game. If you do find yourself in a surprise battle, sprint away and you'll

Recangukan Bamaib

69.3 Tox | 1.2°C
1.0 Rad

get a notification once they've disbanded. They have short memory banks, so you can resume your activities right away.

You may not have had the fortune of starting out in a hospitable place. If that's the case, you'll probably hear status reports about your suit's resources running low while being pelted with toxic rain or risking freezing temperatures. To keep that topped off, open your suit's menu by pressing the touchpad and move the cursor over the hazard protection section of your suit and press X to refuel it with oxides, which are yellow elements such as iron, zinc, and titanium.

Your suit has 12 inventory slots, but three of them are dedicated to critical functions: life support, shielding, and your jet pack. First, that means that you might not want to grab everything within sight, as tempting as it might be. Secondly, you have a jet pack! Hold down the X button to jump, and hold it down to climb. An icon will appear in the lower right, indicating how much jet-pack juice you're using. When it depletes, you could be in for a hard landing, so it's a good idea to mitigate any potential damage by keeping a quarter of your fuel in reserves for reducing the impact of landings. You can also get around faster by sprinting, by pressing R3. Both your sprint power and jet-pack fuel refills over time, so don't be shy about using them.

Your jet pack can also pull off another neat little navigation trick: You can scale incredible heights, regardless of your pack's fuel reserves, if you walk into a cliffside or wall while holding the X button. Even if you're out of fuel, you'll continue to ascend—so don't worry if your ship appears to be impossibly out of reach.

Traintruction

Units: 0

EXOSUIT INVENTORY (12 SLOTS)

Jetpack	Iazard Protecti	
Life Support	Shielding Shar	scination Bead	Plutonium
Iron	Iron	Carite Sheet
Carite Sheet	Carite Sheet	Carite Sheet

[A] EXOSUIT | STARSHIP | MULTI-TOOL [D]

EQUIPMENT
Install technology and manage your exosuit inventory

PR

S

U

RETURN [P]

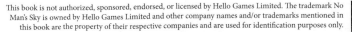

One last note on inventory space: you actually have more than you might assume. Once your suit's stash is filled, you'll see a red shield-shaped icon appear in the bottom-right side of your HUD. Pop into your suit's inventory screen, and you'll be able to do another nifty trick. You can shuttle away items in your personal inventory to your ship thanks to some kind of space sorcery. Just hover the items you want to pass along and press the triangle button. They'll be whisked over to your ship, no matter how much distance there is between you. You will need to be closer to the ship for the transaction to work the other way, though. Elements stack in clusters of 250 units in your suit, but they top off at 500 items per stack in your ship's holds. As you can see, it makes sense to take advantage of that additional trunk space whenever possible.

It's a good idea to repair your multi-tool as soon as you can, so once you have acquired the necessary carbon and iron, pull up your inventory by pressing the touchpad button on the controller. You'll see different sections for your suit, ship, and multi-tool. Use the L1 and R1 buttons to navigate to the multi-tool section, and then move the cursor over the boxes that are marked with exclamation points. Those are the broken pieces of equipment. Hover the cursor each one, and repair them by holding down X.

Repairing the ship components is a similar process, but there's an intermediate step. First, you need to craft additional carite sheets. To do that, pick an empty slot on your ship's inventory and press the square button. From the sub menu that pops up, select carite sheets, and craft those. Once you have created enough—four

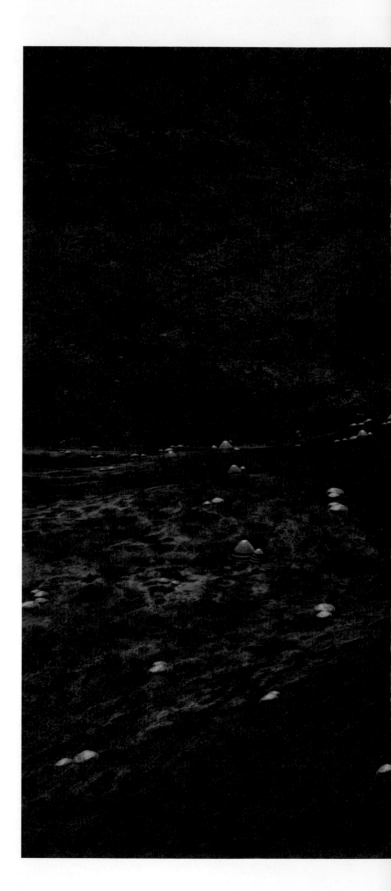

Teleport items from Exosuit to Starship at any time
Press [X] in your Inventory [Tab]

Traintruction

Units: 0 ⊕

STARSHIP INVE

LAUNCH THRUST
Vertical Take-off System

Vital launch and landing gear s

User is advised that Plutonium
Launch procedures require su
activation.

Hold [W] to take off from plane
Hold [Space] to initiate in-flight s

❶ This technology

Repair

Carite Sheet
Craft products in inventor

🔧 REPAIR
Repair this technology

iunch Thruster

hoton Cannon

Carite Sheet

Ⓐ EXOSUIT | STARSHIP | MULTI-TOOL Ⓓ

Rasamama S

Install technology and manage your starship's c

n.

quired to recharge thruster.
t fuel levels before

boost.

tically damaged ❗

4 of 4 ✔

RETURN Ⓟ

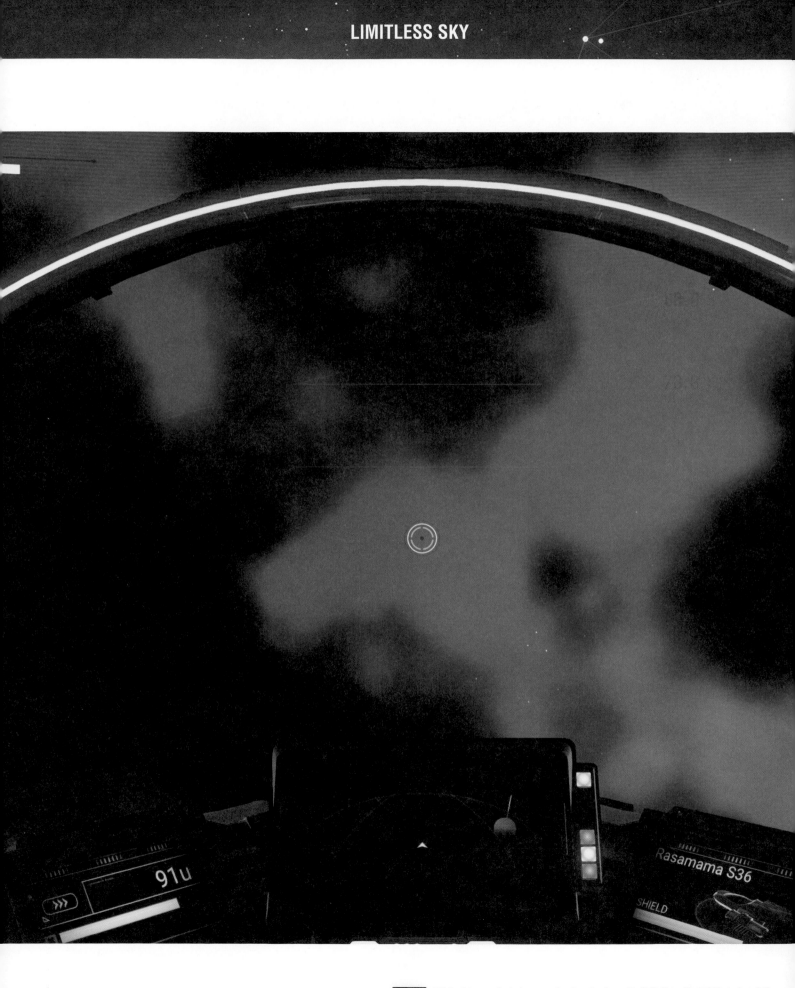

100%

PHOTON CANNON

Leave Planet
Repair Launch Thrusters ✓
Repair Pulse Engine ✓
Refuel Launch Thrusters ✓

Photon Cann

for the launch thruster and two for the pulse engine—you can repair those components the same way you did for the multi-tool. If you select the repaired launch thruster, you'll see an option to fuel it. Choose it, and drop some of your plutonium into it—you have been collecting that, right?

At this point, you can now leave the planet. Before you do, be sure to check out your multi-tool's restored functionality. L3 performs a scan of the area, highlighting nearby points of interest, such as resources and items, with icons for a short period of time. Holding L2 lets you use your analysis visor, which is used to scan plants, rocks, and animals, adding them to your database. We'll dive deeper into that aspect of the game a bit later, but you should definitely scan anything that looks interesting in the meantime.

Once you're ready to say good-bye to your first planet, it's time to get in your ship and take off. Leaving can be hard, especially if you liked your starting location. One of the things you need to keep in mind with No Man's Sky is that there are always more planets to explore, and that you can't possibly see everything. The sooner you come to terms with that harsh reality, the better.

Ready to go? Get in your ship, hold down the right trigger, aim up, and blast off.

JOURNEY MILESTO

E ACCOMPLISHED

GOING OFFWORLD

All right! You're in space. Let's try not to crash again, all right?

You'll notice that the game's controls change in some fundamental ways when you're flying. The triggers now control your thrusters, with R2 providing acceleration and L2 slowing your down. The bumper buttons rotate your ship left and right. Since the triggers are being used for other things, you can fire your weapon by pressing X. If you like the controls, great. You might find yourself annoyed by how up and down function, particularly if you play a lot of flight-based games. In that case, head over to the options menu and invert your flight controls. Don't worry, we won't judge.

Now that you're in space, take the opportunity to blast apart some asteroids. You'll notice that most of the smaller ones will give you thamium9, which is the primary fuel for your ship's pulse engine. Once you've acquired some of that, head into your ship's inventory and refuel it. Once that's done, you can

now activate your pulse engines by pressing the left and right bumpers simultaneously—provided you're far away enough from the planet's surface. If you get a warning about planetary interference, simply aim your ship up. You have an intermediate booster at your disposal, too, which is mapped to the circle button. Unlike the pulse engines, you can use that to get around faster when you're exploring a planet in your ship.

Your ship is also equipped with a scanner, though it's slower to recharge than your multi-tool's tech. It does scan an entire planet, however, so we'll cut it a little slack. Scan the planets around you, and you'll see points of interest pop up on their surface.

You'll also notice an indicator that there's a beacon on a planet. Head in that direction to continue along what's called the Atlas path.

By now, you've probably noticed that No Man's Sky measures distance by estimated time of arrival as opposed to miles or kilometers. It's a handy way to see just how much of a time commitment you'll be making by following an indicator on the horizon. A two-minute hike might be worth the reward, but if it's going to take 20 minutes, it may be better to hop into your ship. That way of measuring distance is also a powerful way to convey just how fast your ship is able to travel. Just for fun, take a look at the beacon from a stop and hover your

ship's targeting reticle over it. Now take off using your regular engines. See how the estimated time shrinks? It's still a long ways away, more than likely. Watch it shrink further by adding boosters to the mix. Finally, activate your pulse engines and watch the time melt away. It still may take a minute or so, but it beats walking. There's an even faster way of getting around, which is what we're building up to.

When your ship breaks through a planet's atmosphere, you may notice that the game looks a little weird and hazy, particularly when you're going fast, especially around the horizon. That's the game's engine building the world around you on the fly. From your cockpit, you'll be able to make out large formations such as outposts, crashed ships, large elemental deposits, cave entrances, and a plethora of other interesting stuff. You won't, however, be able to see most of the plant life or any animals from your ship, which is something you should keep in mind when you approach a planet for the first time. What may seem completely devoid of life from inside your ship may actually be bustling with activity. If you never got out, you may never find out.

When you get close to the beacon, slow down and press square to land. You should optimally find a flat spot, or as flat a place as possible, but the game simply won't allow you to land if you're trying to touch down on someplace that's a little too rocky or crazy. Your ship's also smart enough to prevent you from crashing into cliffs, rock structures, and other obstacles, so feel free to fly like a maniac.

After landing, you'll get the planet's vital statistics, which are incredibly important to know. Just as you don't get a sense of what's going on with a planet's wildlife from the comfort of your cockpit, you won't completely understand what a planet's composition is like until you land. When you do, you'll learn about the planet's climate or hazards, as well as the levels of its flora (plants) and fauna (animals). You'll also get a heads up on how active a planet's Sentinels are, from passive to hostile. Planets that have hostile Sentinels and inhospitable climates also hold the potential of better resources, so there's a definite risk/reward balance if you can stay alive long enough to harvest the benefits.

The beacon will direct you to an alien lifeform who needs your help. You'll need to head toward that new waypoint to progress on the path.

But—and this is critically important—you're absolutely free to wander and explore as you see fit.

When you talk to the alien, you'll be given some kind of randomized scenario. You don't have much in the way of a common tongue at this point, but we'll get your linguistics skills honed. Meanwhile, choose an option that seems most beneficial to the creature, and you should be rewarded with blueprints to build a hyperdrive for your ship. Now we're talking.

You may have already picked up some blueprints by now, from the wrecked machinery in the initial crash site, or from your own exploration. The process of building them works identically to how you repair things, with one critical difference: your three inventories have limited space, and blueprints will take up one slot. When you're starting out, space is critically important, so you might want to hold off

instead of building everything that comes your way. A hyperdrive is a must-have accessory for your ship, though, so let's work on gathering the necessary components.

To build a hyperdrive, you need to acquire more heridium and something called a dynamic resonator. You'll eventually get a blueprint to craft the latter item, but for now you may need to open up your space wallet. Before we move on, you might want to gather as much plutonium and iron as your inventories can hold, making sure to fill your ship's inventory space as well. Trust us.

Ready to move on? Blast off and out of the atmosphere, and look around for a space station. Aim your ship's nose at it, and activate your pulse engine. Don't worry—your ship will automatically detect an imminent collision and stop the engines before you splat into the station's side. You should see a blue beam indicating the station's entrance. Fly into it, and you'll head inside.

Space stations are great places to visit, which is probably why every solar system in the galaxy has one. While their exteriors can vary, you'll notice that the interiors are quite similar. If your back is to the exit, you'll see elevated doors on your left and right. The right side will lead you to a variety of important services. The left side, alas, is locked. Don't worry, we'll get the keycard for that eventually. In the meantime, you'll have to imagine what's on the other side.

The open area where you're standing is where other ships come and go. You can interact with their pilots and trade with them, but for now, let's go deeper inside the station.

Once you go through the doors on the right, you'll likely see another strange alien behind a desk. Interact with it, and get a nice reminder of the language barrier. Your initial interaction will usually play out with some kind of multiple-choice scenario, and picking the right option—either through dialogue or selecting an appropriate gift from your inventory—can result in significant rewards. Even if you fail, there are plenty of aliens and space stations in the galaxy. It never hurts to try.

Along the wall, you'll notice a circular interface. That's the trade terminal, which you can use to buy and sell items. These are important, particularly in the beginning of the game. Interact with it, and choose the buy option. There should be an option to purchase a dynamic resonator, though it might be a little pricy depending on how the economy is working at the moment.

You filled your inventory with iron and platinum, right? If you don't mind some repetition, there's a sneaky way to get a bunch of money early on. Go into your suit's inventory and craft a bypass chip. These items can be constructed with a paltry 10 platinum and 10 iron, but they sell for more than 3,000 Units apiece—the game's currency. That's significantly more than the elements themselves are worth, which is why building and selling these can be so lucrative. It's tedious, but it's also a surefire way to get the cash you need to get that dynamic resonator. If that doesn't seem like an enjoyable way to spend your time, you can also sell stacks of elements or items marked as trade commodities,

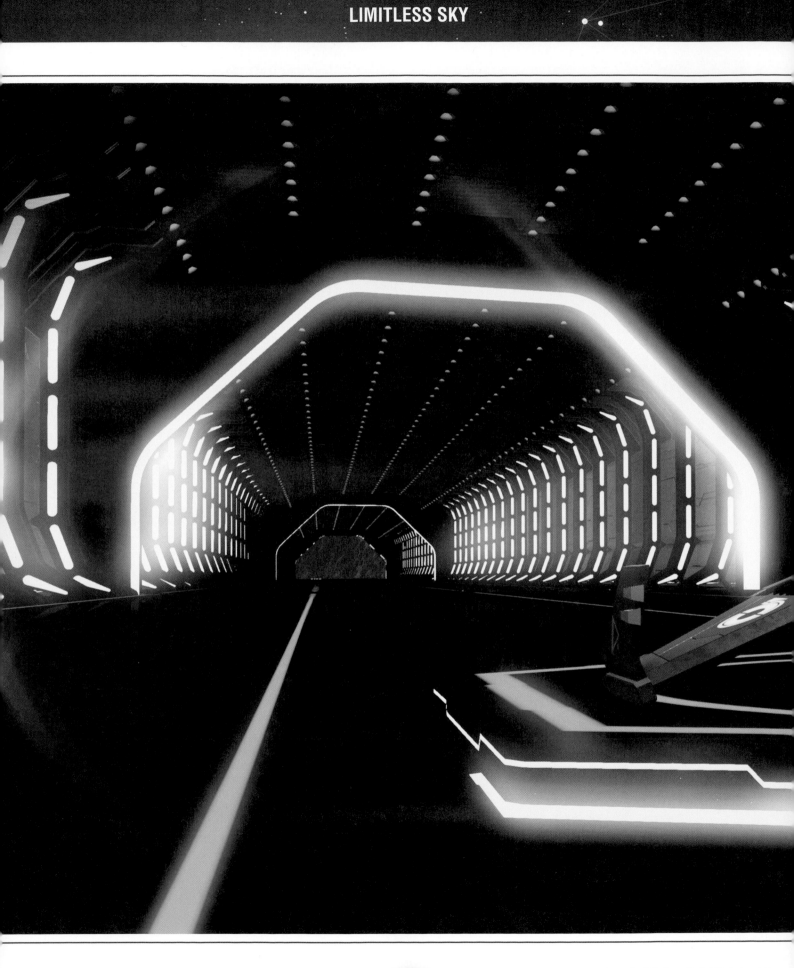

like beads and figurines, that serve few other purposes.

Your next move, after installing the hyperdrive, will be tracking down the warp cells that are necessary to fuel the device—it doesn't run on dreams, after all. Crafting warp cells is one of the game's biggest loops, so you should get used to this process sooner rather than later. You'll get the recipe, but you won't be able to craft antimatter, which is a

required component. You can buy it from most trade terminals, but it's expensive. You'll also need suspension fluid, which you can buy if you don't yet have the recipe.

Ultimately, here's the crafting path for warp cells, so you can keep these elements in mind while you explore:

▶ Warp core: Electron vapour (1), zinc (20), heridium (50)

1702 - 7021 - 0217 - ✱✱✱✱

Ajrapioru Reflector
Vy'keen Observatory

► Electron vapour: Suspension fluid (1), plutonium (100)

► Suspension fluid: Carbon (50)

You probably noticed that every item requires one component that's built from the lower tier, starting with suspension fluid. Again, you can buy suspension fluid, but you can get the recipe relatively easily and save the Units. When you're on a planet, keep an eye out for a signal scanner.

They're stout little objects that fire a beam of amber light into the sky. Craft and use a bypass chip on it (those chips have an actual purpose, believe it or not), and select "Colonial Outpost" from the four options that appear. If it directs you to a manufacturing facility, head to the waypoint. Otherwise, repeat the process until it does.

Once you get there, you'll see that the doors are locked. Your multi-tool's mining beam is worthless

beacon sent long ago from a distant system awaits my response.

ee numbers are visible above an empty input box. I think I know what comes next...

ut: 1702

ut: 1720

ut: 2170

Q ⊚ • • •   E

Path towards galactic core

⟨ ● ⟩   ✦ Attealliude-Puyor XIX
REGION : Gegsakoongba Adjunct

ANALYSIS
Class G3pf // 5 Planets

DISCOVERED BY
You, on 8/12/2016 (13:19)

DISTANCE TO CENTRE
175986.8 Light-years

WARP UNNECESSARY
CURRENT LOCATION

[Tab] SCAN FOR DISCOVERIES   🖮 ROTATE 🖱 PUSH SELECT 🖱 DESELECT

here, so you're going to need to upgrade it with either a boltcaster or plasma grenades. Plasma grenades are the best option, all things being equal. Blueprints for multi-tool upgrades are typically found in shelters and small buildings, via wall-mounted dispensers. They're randomized, so you may have to do some hunting to get the upgrade you want.

Once you've upgraded your tool, fire a few grenades at the door with L1 until the door blasts open. You'll likely attract the attention of some angry Sentinels at this point, but you can simply duck inside and they'll go away. Once in, you need to interact with the terminal and solve a multiple-

choice problem from a randomized pool to get a blueprint. Odds are, if you already have built a hyperdrive and the warp-cell recipe, you'll get the one for suspension fluid. Otherwise, try again.

Have you built your warp cell? Good! Use it to fuel your hyperdrive unit in your ship's inventory, the same way you've been fueling your ship's pulse engines. While in space, you'll see an indicator to press down on the d-pad to open up the galactic map. Do that.

The map shows you a zoomed-out version of the galaxy. See that little dot at the start? That's the solar system you've been exploring. Suddenly,

everything seems so small. You'll see a connecting line between some of the stars, guiding you toward your destination. You can follow that path by aiming toward the connecting line with the right stick. Go as far as you can—the window will tell you when you're out of range for your current hyperdrive. Once you've maxed out your distance, press the button to warp.

Once the light show is over, you're in a whole new solar system. You'll get a waypoint leading you to a manufacturing facility, and you should prioritize that visit. It will lead you to the recipe for antimatter, which as you know is a vital link in the

warp-cell chain. Once you procure that recipe—in a process remarkably similar to how you may have grabbed the ability to craft suspension fluid—you've completed one of the game's biggest loops.

From here, you're probably getting a good sense of how your exploration fuels your travels (quite literally), which in turn leads to more exploration. Over the next few chapters, we're going to take a moment to dive into your equipment, since you've been using it for a while now. In the meantime, congratulate yourself on your first big steps, and celebrate by seeing some things that nobody has ever seen before.

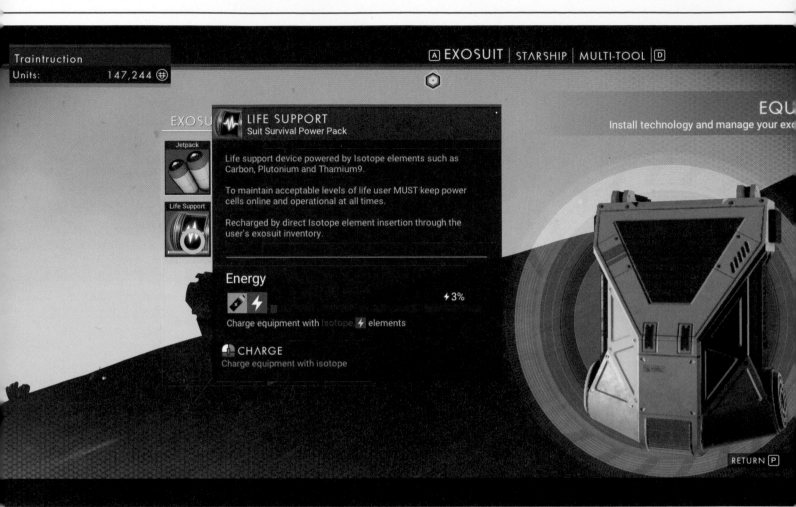

Traintruction
Units: 147,244

Ⓐ EXOSUIT | STARSHIP | MULTI-TOOL Ⓓ

EXOSU

EQU
Install technology and manage your exc

Jetpack

Life Support

LIFE SUPPORT
Suit Survival Power Pack

Life support device powered by Isotope elements such as
Carbon, Plutonium and Thamium9.

To maintain acceptable levels of life user MUST keep power
cells online and operational at all times.

Recharged by direct Isotope element insertion through the
user's exosuit inventory.

Energy

⚡3%

Charge equipment with Isotope ⚡ elements

CHARGE
Charge equipment with isotope

RETURN Ⓟ

YOUR SUIT

Your suit is the only thing that keeps you from
crisping up like a fritter in the heat or having your
blood freeze into slush on the other extreme.

(At least, we assume you have blood. You never get
confirmation of what exactly you are, aside from
knowing that you're some kind of bipedal creature.
Regardless, we do know that you have a suit.)

In addition to providing a barrier between you and
unforgiving worlds, your suit also governs how much
stuff you can carry. As we mentioned earlier, you

can transfer items from your personal inventory over
to your ship using some kind of space magic, but it's
always handy to have additional carrying capacity.

When you start out, those nine free slots seem like
a respectable amount. After tromping around for
a while, you'll realize just how limiting it can be.
There's a lot of potential for your suit's capacity, and
determined players can fully kit it out with 48 slots.
That sounds like a lot—and it is—but keep in mind
that by the time you get to that point in the game, at

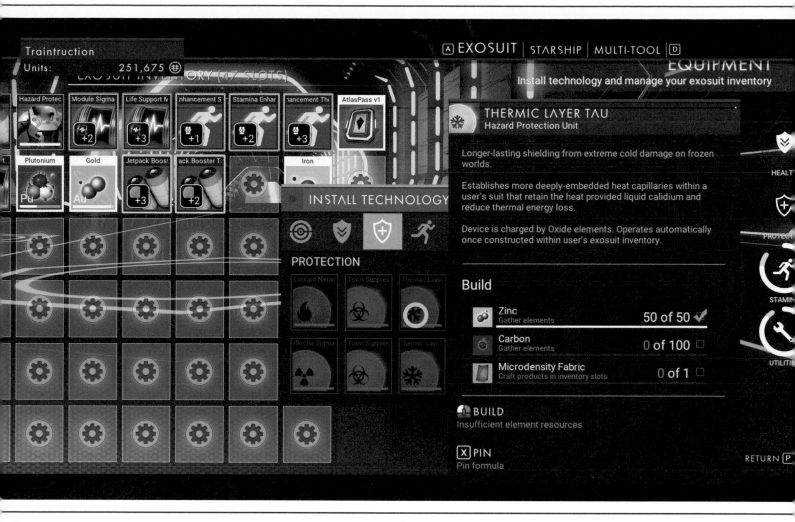

least some of those slots are going to be devoted to suit upgrades.

As we said before, you're going to have to strike a balance in your game between being able to carry enough items for your trips to remain lucrative, and being able to survive long enough during those trips to squirrel away that loot. When you're on a planet that has a midday temperature that approaches the boiling point, your default gear isn't going to cut it.

First, let's focus on getting you some additional slots for your suits. During your travels, you may have already stumbled upon something called a

drop pod. These single-person (or whatever it is that you are) shelters provide a temporary respite from extreme conditions. They also will let you upgrade your suit by one slot—for a price. The first one will cost 10,000 Units, and subsequent upgrades increase in price until the final one, which will set you back a cool 350,000 Units.

Finding drop pods can be simplified if you use the signal scanners, which are scattered across planets. Using a bypass chip—an item you can craft from the start—allows you to ping the environment for a type of building. Selecting "shelter" can possibly pull up a drop-pod location and put a waypoint on your

STORM

Tutwageschinn

9.8 Rad | 0.8°C 14.7 Tox

HUD. If it doesn't, simply use another bypass unit until it does. If you have a sizeable stash of money and you're looking to buy several upgrades, you can repeat the beacon process multiple times and get several drop-pod locations on your screen. From there, it's simply a matter of jetting around from point to point (and opening your space wallet).

Space stations also have a suit-upgrade dispensary, but they're behind those locked doors that require an Atlas Pass v1. You'll eventually find the

blueprints for those as you progress along the Atlas path, so don't worry.

Once you have some extra space, it's time to consider some of the game's suit upgrades. These require blueprints, which can be found by interacting with panels inside some buildings and shelters or as rewards for some types of alien interactions. Each type of upgrade has several ranks, from the lowly sigma to tau, theta, and omega. Better upgrades often require exotic and expensive materials.

The default sprint is kept on a fairly short leash, but you can equip stamina upgrades to allow your character to run for longer distances before getting exhausted. Similarly, jet-pack upgrades allow you to use that piece of equipment longer before running out of fuel.

You'll also get access to specialized suit upgrades that supplement your suit's default environmental-protection systems. It's tempting to go whole hog on those, but it's wise to resist that urge until you have inventory space to burn. Instead, focus on resistance types for the situation at hand, rotating them in and out as needed. These can be crafted, and then later dismantled with R3 in the inventory screen, so you shouldn't feel locked into any decisions. There's no point in protecting yourself against radiation if the looming threat is instant frostbite, after all. Tailor your kit to whatever you're facing at any given moment—especially if you plan on sticking around on a particularly lucrative (and hazardous) planet.

Traintruction

Units: 251,675 ⊕

EXOSUIT INVENTORY (47 SLOTS)

tpack	Hazard Protec	ort Module Sig	Life Support M	nina Enhancem	tamina Enhanc	na Enhanceme	AtlasPass v1
		+2	+3	+1	+2	+3	
Support	Plutonium	Gold	Booster Theta	k Booster Tau		Iron	
	Pu	Au	+3	+2			

INSTALL TECH

PROTECTION

etwork Sigma | uppressor The

eflector Sigm | pressor Sigma

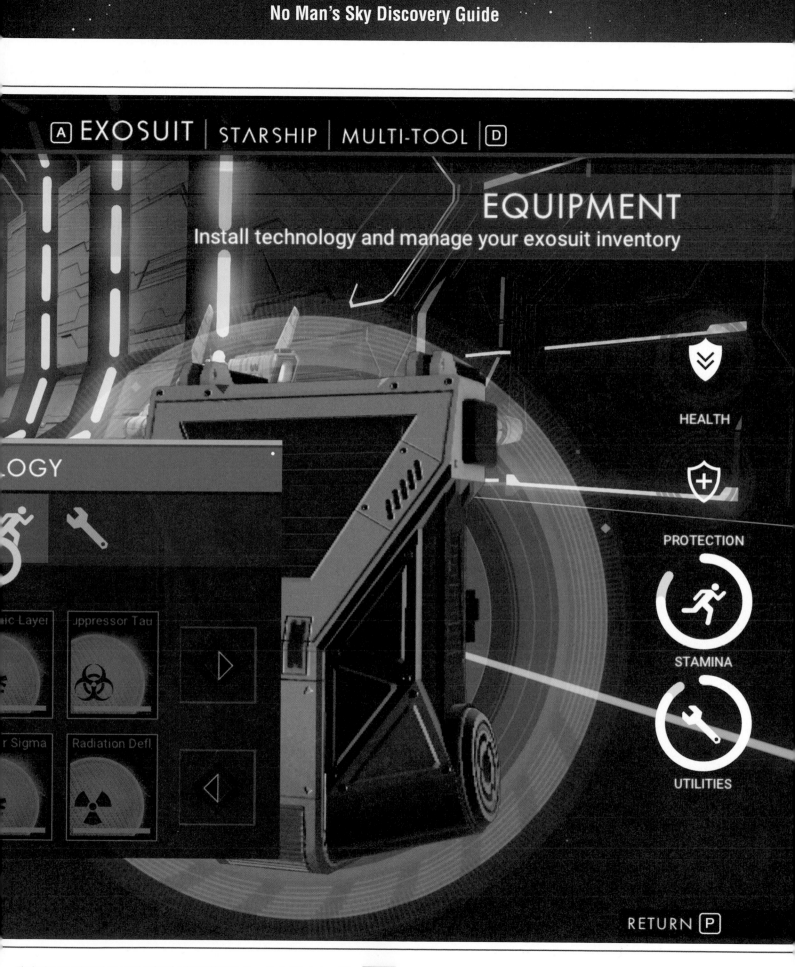

Ⓐ EXOSUIT | STARSHIP | MULTI-TOOL Ⓓ

EQUIPMENT
Install technology and manage your exosuit inventory

HEALTH

PROTECTION

STAMINA

UTILITIES

...OGY

...ic Layer | ...ppressor Tau

...r Sigma | Radiation Defl.

RETURN Ⓟ

YOUR MULTI-TOOL

Your suit and multi-tool are two constants in your journey in No Man's Sky, though the multi-tool is different in one big way: Unlike the suit, you won't be upgrading the starter unit by adding capacity to it. Instead, you'll be replacing the whole thing—unless you like feeling limited.

Let's face it: the first multi-tool is nice, but you're going to outgrow it faster than perhaps any other piece of equipment in the game. It governs your effectiveness in combat, how easily you can terraform the world, and—most importantly—your mining efficiency.

Your initial tool has five slots in it, which is a far cry from the maximum 24-slot beasts that you can eventually acquire. Unlike the suit and ship, which also serve as inventory slots, there's no benefit to keeping empty spots on your multi-tool. You'll want to fill up every available inch with firepower to squeeze the most power from it.

There are three main weapon types in the tool, in addition to its scanning functionality. The mining beam is what you start with, and you can also add plasma grenades and a boltcaster weapon to it once you find the blueprints. From there, additional blueprints decrease load times for weapons, or the beam's focus and intensity for mining.

Combat is, unfortunately, one of the weaker parts of the game, and as such it doesn't make much sense to focus on the boltcaster in the early parts of the game. Instead, a solid choice is to put as many mining-beam upgrades into the device as possible, while keeping one spot open for plasma grenades. Grenades are a great way to blast through

reinforced doors in manufacturing facilities, as well as the most efficient way to mine iron and carbon deposits from large rocks and plants.

If you do decide that you need better protection from creatures and Sentinels than the mining beam can provide, the boltcaster will do the trick. It features a generous aim assist, meaning that you don't need to have your target absolutely centered to make the shot. Mining is a more efficient way to make money and earn resources than hassling the locals, so it makes more sense to focus your early efforts on tools that make that aspect of the game easier. That said, it's nice to be able to take out pesky drones without any trouble, particularly

on planets that have an aggressive Sentinel presence.

Grenades can also blast apart the planetary surface, instead of ricocheting harmlessly like your other weapons. This allows you to carve out caves to take shelter from deadly storms or to create an exit to an existing cave network if you get lost. For that reason alone, they're worth the upgrade slot.

You won't upgrade your multi-tool as a unit, but you'll find replacements during your travels. They can appear as rewards from aliens for picking the right conversation options, as well as from shelves inside buildings. Keep an eye out for small outposts that have a single landing pad. They often contain new multi-tools. Later in the game, you'll run into a space anomaly that contains a guaranteed multi-tool, though it's not always an improvement over what you may have equipped at any moment.

The multi-tool can be recharged from isotopes, which are generally quite common. For that reason—as well as the fact that it's used to fuel your ship's launch thrusters—it's a good idea to keep a stack of plutonium in your suit's inventory, just in case.

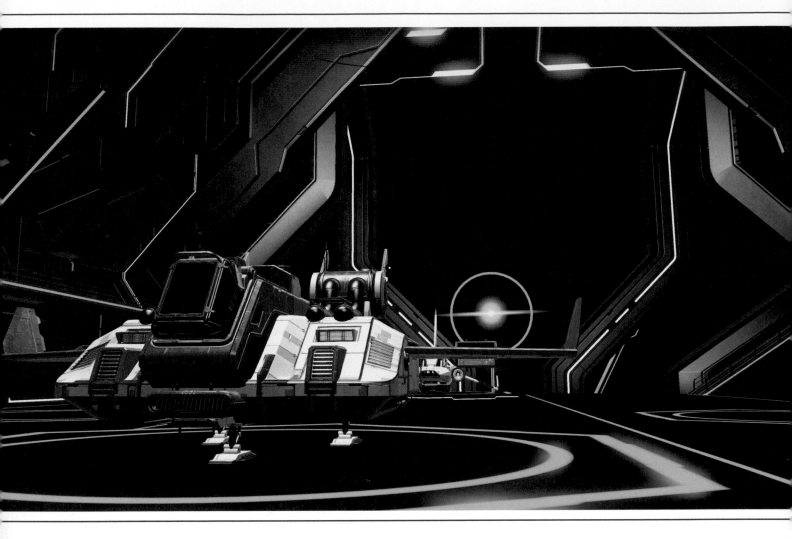

YOUR SHIP

Your suit may provide a layer of protection against the elements and other hazards, but your ship is like an armored vault. When upgraded, it provides a vast hold of storage capacity beneath a thick shell of armor. Your starting vessel may be humble, but if you have the interest and dedication, you can eventually work your way to something akin to a flying Fort Knox—one that's fully decked out in death rays, too.

Are you too hot? Being torn apart at an atomic level from radiation or having your respirator clogged

from toxic gases? Jump into your ship, and you'll be fine. As long as you're inside, you're safe from the effects of just about anything that a planet can throw your way, from hostile creatures and Sentinels to the environment itself. You'll have to reckon with whatever realities you're dealt with once you leave the cockpit, but at least your ship will give you precious time to regroup, craft vital items in safety, and prepare yourself before going back for more. If you get separated from your ship, you can call it back to you by interacting with cylindrical beacons

STORM

∥ Tutwageschinn
0.8°C
14.7 Tox

or the terminals near some outpost landing pads. Don't worry—you can't lose your ship. It's too important.

Your ship's main systems are fueled by two primary elements: plutonium and thamium9. By now, you should know what plutonium looks like: It appears on planetary surfaces as prickly red crystals. Thamium9 is harder to find on the surface—it

appears in red, bulbous clusters—but it's abundant in space. You should make a point of keeping at least a single stack of plutonium in your ship's hold at any time. All planets will have the resources necessary to refuel, but it may require a significant hike to find plutonium. There are fewer things more demoralizing than having to walk 15 minutes, looking for the closest source to top off your tanks.

Every time you take off using your ship's launch thrusters, it takes a fixed amount of your fuel. There is an exception, however. If you can land at a station or outpost that has a designated landing pad, taking off is free—the same goes for space stations. Landing on a pad also has the added bonus of leaving your ship facing the entrance to the structure. It's the little things, sometimes.

Your ship can be equipped with a pair of weapons, and you can switch between them with the triangle button. The photon cannon is a basic energy projectile, capable of tearing asteroids apart with a single barrage. The optional phase beam directs a continuous stream of energy at its target. Both can be used in space combat, and they each have their advantages and disadvantages.

The photon cannon provides an endless supply of firepower—you don't need to worry about running out of ammo. The downside is that you'll need to target enemies manually for it to be effective. When an enemy is within range, you'll see two crosshairs. The smaller one designates the hostile craft, showing where it is. Another one will appear ahead of the ship, predicting where you need to fire to hit the moving vessel. As long as you're close to that target, you should be OK.

The phase beam provides short, intense blasts. It has a tendency to overheat, and it rapidly runs through its isotope fuel. It does automatically target enemies that are within range, though, and it can take smaller ships out quickly. If you plan on spending time in combat, installing and upgrading the phase beam is a no-brainer.

We've covered this before, but it bears repeating. Even if your ship and suit max out at 48 slots, your

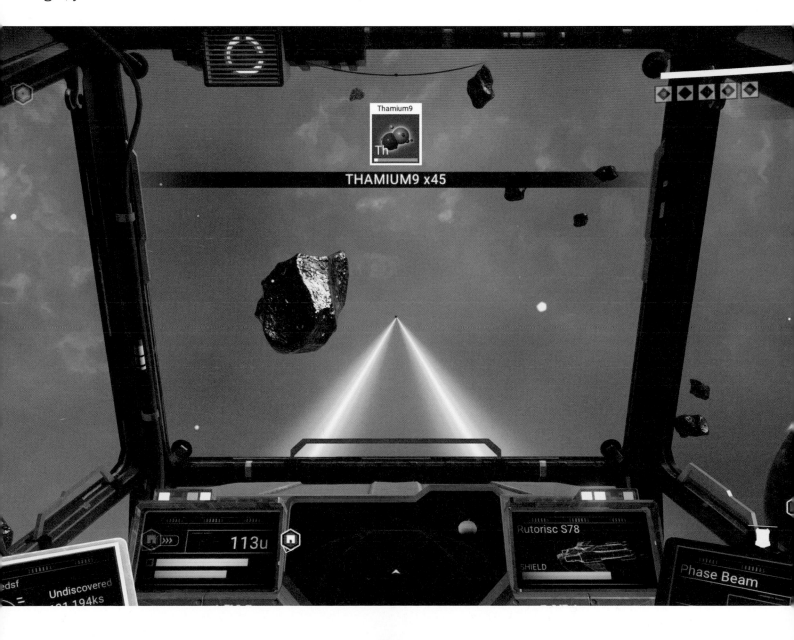

ship can actually hold more elements, pound per pound. The vast majority of elements will arrange themselves in stacks of the same type, until the stack is maxed out. Collect more carbon, and the new supply will be piled onto your existing store of carbon, for example. In your suit, these stacks can contain 250 individual items. On the ship, these stacks max out at 500. Once again, it makes sense to take advantage of your suit's ability to teleport your inventory to the ship whenever possible, because of that difference. An exception can (and should) be made for items like warp cells, which don't stack. If you're running low on storage space in your ship, keep those single items in your suit if possible, and use your ship as a dedicated elemental-storage unit.

Your ship's engines also have several levels. The basic throttle (R2) is certainly faster than walking, but it's slow when considering the great distances that you'll be required to travel. Pressing circle engages a booster, which is the fastest way you can go near a planet's surface. If a waypoint is still minutes away, even with the boost engaged, it makes sense to get away from the planet's surface and engage the pulse engines by pressing L1+R1. Once active, you don't need to hold them down anymore. To cut off the pulse engines, hit the brakes with L2. It's not a bad idea to use your ship's scanning module while you're in space, too. Press the same button as you would on foot (L3) to do a scan and call up points of interest on a planet's surface. It's a great way to get some guidance when you first enter a new solar system.

Planetary interference prevents you from using your ship's pulse engines within a planet's atmosphere, but it apparently causes problems

ARRIVE IN: 0:10
BEACON

Pulse Engine Active

Rasamama S36

SHIELD

Photon Cannon

HEAT

Fuel Remaining

285,543ks

with other systems, too. While skimming a planet's surface in your ship, you may notice large, shiny mineral deposits just begging to be mined. Your ship's weapons are great at reducing asteroids to their elemental building blocks, but they simply won't work on rocks and objects on a planet. For those, you're going to need to park as close as possible and do it the old-fashioned way, using your multi-tool.

Your starter ship is cramped and underpowered, and you'll probably want to start thinking about upgrading it after a couple of hours. There are a couple of ways to do it, and both of them will require a fairly significant time investment. The easiest way is to talk to one of the traders that ferry in and out of space stations. You can start a conversation with the pilots by walking up to their ship's cockpits and interacting with them. The first option that pops up from their menu will allow you to make an offer on their ship. Apparently, they don't mind the thought of being stranded on space stations, since they're all willing to part with their transportation. (Other options will allow you to trade with them, too, but the comparatively lengthy text crawl that appears with these interactions makes the terminals inside a more efficient way to repeatedly buy and sell items.)

It's not a bad idea to save enough cash—either by mining resources or crafting and selling bypass chips—to purchase a ship with 24 or so slots. That should set you back several million units, but it's a worthy investment. Don't let looks mislead you, either. Ships may look small, but they might surprise you with how much they can haul. Other than cosmetics and carrying capacity, ships are functionally identical, so you can let aesthetics be your deciding factor if you'd like.

The cheaper way, at least as far as units are concerned, will take a while. It does pay off, however, since you'll end up with a maxed-out ship without spending a space dime. Not too shabby. Even if you decide to go this route, you should start by buying a larger ship. It will eliminate at least some of the tedium that's coming your way, and the extra space will let you carry some of the valuable resources you can acquire during the process.

On your travels, you may have come across the remains of a crashed ship. Unlike you, resourceful traveler that you are, these ships were destined to remain marooned forever. You fixed a battered wreck before, and you can do it again—over and over and over again, in fact! To start this process,

head to a signal scanner on a planet's surface and use a bypass chip. Have it search for transmissions. You're looking for transmission towers, so repeat the process until one pops up. Once it does, get in your ship and head toward the newly discovered waypoint.

Once you're there, go inside the building and interact with the terminal. You'll be asked to solve a puzzle, where you have to select the number that completes a pattern. Most of these are incredibly simple to solve. Here's a tip that will let you blow past the majority of them: the first number contains the entire sequence, so look at it. The next number will likely repeat the same sequence, but offset by one number. That will continue with the third, and

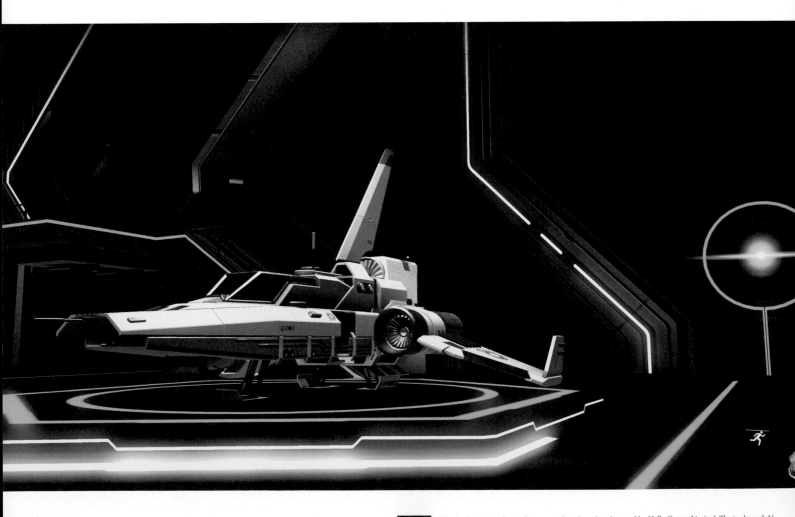

then all you need to do is plug in the fourth one. Like so: 9368 3689 6893 ____. In this example, the correct option would be 8936. Essentially, they're on a loop, and you just need to cycle through.

After solving the puzzle, the terminal will tell you that it's discovered a transmission signal from a crashed ship. Great! If you discovered several transmission towers earlier, be sure to visit those before heading out.

When you get to the crash site, you have several things to do. You can plunder some blueprints from the wrecked machinery that's almost always there, as well as interact with its beacon pod. The pods will create little scenarios for you, which have multiple-choice options. Be bold—you may take small hits to

your health now and then, but taking risks can result in some nice rewards along the way. So investigate that sound and check out that creepy altar (these will make more sense when you're playing).

Then it's time to look at the ship itself. Interact with it, and keep an eye on its inventory space. Is it higher than what you have? Awesome! Transfer your stuff over to the bigger ship, and you're done. You'll get used to the smell of smoke and alien skeletons. If it's the same size or smaller, you can still dismantle most of the ship's upgrades by moving your cursor over them and holding down R3. You can score some great crafting materials and stacks of rare elements doing this, so be sure to do it with your old ship's parts, too. New ships are generated

LUKNA:0D0A:0085:0CAB:0044
Interact // Signal Scanner
1x Bypass Chip required

Gelsehan GZ585
6.6°C 0.0 Rad

Traintruction

Units: 91,242 ⊕

STARSHIP INVENTORY (48 SLOTS)

Phase Beam	Photon Canno	Deflector Shie	Pulse Engine	Hyperdrive	aunch Thruster	Warp Reactor	Coolant S +1
Deflection Enh +1	Impact Sigma +2	Cannon Dama +1	m Impact Tau +3	ase Coolant Ta +2	Cannon Dama +2	Accelerated Fi +1	Deflection +1
Damage Theta +3	Reactor Theta	on Enhanceme +1	Photonix Core	Accelerated Fi +3	Advanced Coo +1	d Cooling Tau +2	Advance +3
Phase Coolan	p Reactor Tau	Pulse Jet Tau	Accelerated Fi +2	lse Jet Sigma	Beam Impact T +4	Thamium9 Th	hrysor Ch
Iron Fe	Zinc Zn	Aluminium Al	Chrysonite Ch	Thamium9 Th	Thamium9 Th	Aluminium Al	Omeg Om
⚙	⚙	⚙	Iridium Ir	Dimensional M	⚙	Iridium Ir	Alumin Al

Ⓐ EXOSUIT | STARSHIP | MULTI-TOOL Ⓓ

Rutorisc S78
Install technology and manage your starship's cargo

WEAPONS

HEALTH

SCAN

HYPERDRIVE

RETURN Ⓟ

with cargo space that's either the same or a slot or two more or less than what you currently are using. That's why starting out with a 24-slot ship will save you time.

Once you've scavenged everything, it's time to move on to the next ship. You'll have to repair the thrusters and pulse engines first, though, since it did crash for a reason. It's a good idea to make sure you have lots of iron in reserves for the necessary carite sheets. Don't bother fixing any of the other systems, since most of these ships are beaters that are just going to take you to the next, best thing.

After you've investigated all the crash sites, go to a beacon and start over. It will take about three or so hours to find a 48-slot ship, so you might want to do this over the course of several sessions.

Your ship's hyperdrive makes space travel much less of a headache, but it still has its limitations. That's where warp-reactor upgrades come in. After finding these blueprints or getting them from a successful alien interaction, you can add these boosters to your ship. They'll allow you to travel farther with each jump on the galactic map, and also access better classes of star systems. If you've explored the galaxy a bit in the map's free-exploration setting, you've probably been told you need to upgrade your drive. This is what they're talking about. Like multi-tool upgrades, these come in theta, tau, and omega versions, which will in turn let you fly into more exotic star systems.

Arumnacigu YO900

Undiscovered
1,581,020ks

EXPLORING THE WORLD AROUND YOU

While there are plenty of forks in the road to explore, one thing should be clear: exploration is the interstellar freeway that runs through the whole of No Man's Sky. Mining, learning language, even blasting apart and plundering other ships—they all feed into your ability to move from where you are to a whole new world to explore.

You're free to take a meandering route, which has its benefits and drawbacks. On one hand, it's a great game when you have a set amount of time and don't have any particular goals in mind. That kind of open-ended structure (pardon the oxymoron) can be paralyzing, however. Where should you go? What should you look for when you're out and about? What the heck are you supposed to be doing in this game, anyway? We can't possibly catalogue everything there is to do, but we can help to fill out the loops that you've probably started to notice.

When you first land on a new planet, you should take in your surroundings. What's the climate like?

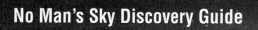

Sentinels
Destroy drones before they alert others
Or avoid detection to escape

Are there any big environmental hazards that you need to take into consideration? How much wildlife can you expect to see? This information will show up when you first land, but you can also get a refresher by going into the options and looking at the planet data.

You've almost certainly noticed those floating, drone-like orbs during your travels. These are Sentinels, and they're a common presence throughout the galaxy. They're so important to the game's overarching ecosystem that they're called out specifically in that planetary-information blurb. Depending on their aggression level—from passive to hostile—they'll react differently to your presence. Passive units will ignore you unless you shoot them with your multi-tool or harvest certain rare materials. Hostile units, on the other hand, will fire at you the moment they notice you. They'll lose interest in you quickly if you sprint away for a bit, so don't worry.

If a drone catches you while you're mining, you'll hear a telltale whirring sound. That's your cue to pause until they go away, if you don't want any trouble. Otherwise, you can shoot them with any of your multi-tool's weapons to enter combat. If you don't take the first one out quickly enough, it will call in reinforcements. As you battle, your notoriety level on the upper right of the HUD will rise, and larger units will be called in—four-legged beasts and two-legged walkers. They all hit hard, but can be taken out with relative ease using the boltcaster or plasma grenades. You can earn resources like titanium from defeating Sentinels, and get blueprints from looting the canisters they drop after dying.

Animals are another potential threat. If you're on a planet that's populated with critters—and not all are—they'll either ignore you or decide that you look delicious. You can tell when you're about to become lunch when a red paw-print icon pops up on your screen. That indicates the direction that the threat is coming from. These beasts can hit hard, surprising you with how quickly they tear through your shield and deplete your health. At this point in the game's life, a glitch allows them to attack you even if you use your jet pack to get out of reach, and some creatures can keep up with your sprint. Your best bet in that case is to go on the offensive with your multi-tool.

You can't ride animals, but they're not entirely window dressing. They're a surprising source of cash, and tracking them down can be profitable if you're patient. When you scan creatures with your analysis visor (L2), you'll get a HUD indicator showing that they're being analyzed. Once a new creature has been identified, it's automatically added to your database and you get a small amount of units. If you do a scan, you can see white dots indicating creatures that are out of range. When you're looking to track down life, these are great beacons. Animals that have small green dots beneath them in the scan view have already been added to your database, while red ones are new to you.

You'll get notifications of how close you are to finding every type of wildlife as you scan new ones. The last few are almost always the trickiest to find, but sometimes it's just a matter of knowing where to look. If your planet has oceans and other large bodies of water, take a quick dip and see if there are any fish around. And don't forget to look up! There are plenty of flying creatures. Those can be tough to scan, so you may have to shoot one down with your multi-tool and scan its corpse. Just tell yourself that it's for science, if that makes you squeamish.

Once you manage to scan every species of creature on a planet, you can get a cash bonus of several hundred thousand Units. Rocks and plants don't count toward the 100-percent completion bonus, but they will earn you money. That initial income isn't the end of it, either. If you go into your database with the options button, you'll see a list of your discoveries, flagged with red checkmarks. You can upload them to the online database with the press of a button, and future explorers (aka other players) will see that you first made those discoveries if they happen to land on the planet. You can upload them with the default name, or you can choose to be creative and come up with your own name for your findings—including planets and solar systems!

Neutral

LIMITLESS SKY

Your multi-tool's scanner is a handy tool, and you should make a habit of regularly performing a scan with L3. You'll see icons that will call out nearby sources of elements and other points of interest. Keep an eye out for gray icons, which indicate crystal formations of valuable elements, and green icons with exclamation points. The latter will direct you to extremely valuable trade commodities, though Sentinels will immediately go on the offensive when you pick them up. They'll cause a bit of a fight, but it's worth the trouble. Circular icons with question marks will point out nearby points of interest, such as outposts and other structures.

You won't need a scanner to find other interesting things. Knowledge stones are easy-to-spot cylinders that will teach you a word in an alien tongue. Wreckage is marked with telltale plumes of smoke and flashing light, and you can typically loot these pods for blueprints. Beacons are clusters of four cylindrical tubes that beam an amber light into the skies above them. They'll point out an alien-populated building that you can investigate if you interact with it. Signal scanners are similar, in that they're machines that emit amber light. They have one major difference, however: you can use a bypass chip on them to ping the nearby environment for specific types of buildings and objects that you're seeking.

Here are the signal-scanner options:

Monoliths

These will direct you to sites that will teach you words in alien languages—important information to have as you interact with aliens more frequently. They can include monoliths and plaques. Monoliths can give you special items and blueprints if you answer their challenges correctly. These multiple-choice tests can be tricky to answer if you don't yet have a beefed-up vocabulary, but it typically pays off to take bold and honorable choices. Be sure to check out the knowledge stones that are around these larger sites. There are usually three nearby, which will show up as purple icons if you use your portable scanner. Plaques will give you additional information about alien races and lore.

Colonial Outposts

If you want to interact with alien technology, these are a safe bet. They'll point you to manufacturing facilities or operations centers. There's a good chance that whoever was there last locked the door behind them, so be prepared to blast it down. Once inside, you can interact with a terminal and solve another multiple-choice problem—usually focused on the structure's security system or automation functionality. Succeed, and you'll get valuable blueprints.

Transmission

This is a great option if you're looking to upgrade your ship at no cost, as outlined in the Your Ship section of this book. Transmission towers will lead you to an outpost with a computer that, once a numeric puzzle is solved, will direct you to a crashed ship. Other options include observatory, which will point you toward a ruin, a site that's similar in function to an alien plaque. Finally, beacons will direct you to the closest populated structure—a boon if you're looking to trade or upgrade your multi-tool.

Shelters

Shelters are a great way to find respite from the elements. They can come in several forms, from the relatively barren generic "shelter," to the more interesting drop pods. The latter is where you can upgrade your suit's carrying capacity, which we covered in the chapter about your suit. Ordinary shelters aren't particularly interesting, but the small structures are worth visiting for their multi-tool upgrade blueprints and stations for charging your health and shields.

An easy way to find places to investigate, and one that doesn't require any bypass chips, is to keep an eye out for other ships or their contrails in the sky. You can follow them, and they will often head toward trade outposts and other populated areas.

Mining can be meditative and relaxing, but there may come a time where you just want to get resources and you don't mind being a scoundrel. In that case, find an area with a landing pad. When ships approach, you can shoot them down and grab whatever cargo they were carrying at the time. You can do the same in space, too, and target smaller

ships and larger freighters. This isn't the smartest way to gain resources if you're looking for particular elements for crafting, since you won't know exactly what kind of loot you'll be grabbing. But, if you don't mind being ruthless, it's certainly an option. Just be prepared for a big fight if you take on larger ships—and expect to meet the equivalent of the space police.

Saving

No Man's Sky is about exploration, but exploring the same thing again because the game crashed or there was a power outage can be a drag. There's not a way to manually save the game in a menu, but you're able to regularly back up your progress. You'll find a pylon near most points of interest, and that will save your game as well as add that location to your list of discoveries. You ship is also a portable save-game station. Whenever you hop out, it'll create a new save for you—so you can simply jump in and jump out, even if you aren't planning on leaving the ground. The game keeps several saves in a rotating order, so if you make a colossal mistake and sell something you didn't mean to, you can possibly roll back your progress by checking out one of the earlier saves.

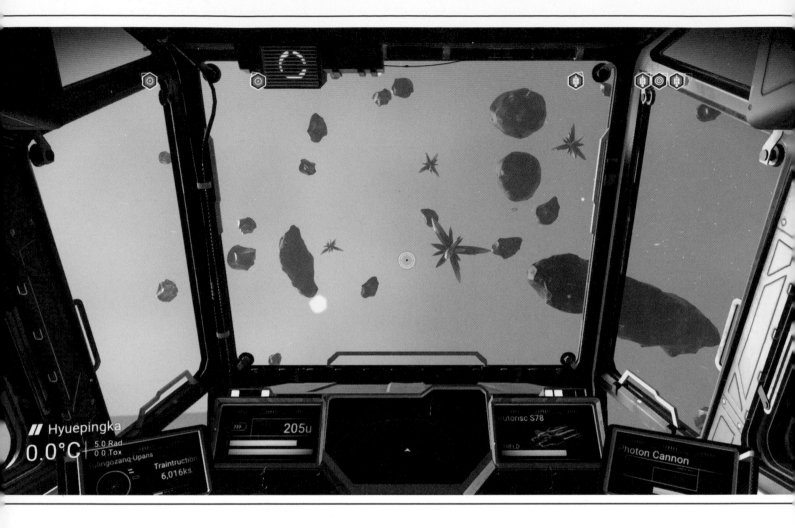

Hyuepingka
0.0°C | 5.0 Rad
0.0 Tox
lingozanq-Upans
Traintruction
6,016ks
205u
utorisc S78
HIELD
Photon Cannon

THE ELEMENTS

Over the course of your journey in No Man's Sky, you're bound to become familiar with a variety of different elements. They're not only the building blocks of all matter—they're an essential part of the game. They're what you mine, what you use to craft and repair your tools, and what you use to line your pockets at the Galactic Trade Network.

Keeping track of all these resources can be a little intimidating at first, but they're organized in a way that makes it easy to understand—once you figure

it out, of course. Here's a rundown of the elements you'll find across the galaxy, along with their per-unit value and what they're typically used for.

Isotopes

Isotopes are the workhorses in No Man's Sky, providing power to your ship, multi-tool, and life support. It's only fitting then that they're represented by a red icon emblazoned with a lightning bolt. In spite of what their descriptions

might lead you to believe, they're all easy to find in the world or in space.

Carbon (Common) 6.9

If it lives, chances are it'll turn into carbon when you blast it with your multi-tool. That means mushrooms, trees, plants, flying lizards, trotting herbivores—all of these will be converted into piles of carbon when you zap them.

Thamium9 (Uncommon) 20.6 plants, asteroids

Thamium9 can be hard to find on planets, where it appears in red plants, but it's impossible to miss it in space. Most asteroids are actually chunks of Thamium9, which is great since it's used to power your ship's pulse engines.

Plutonium (Rare) 41.3

Want to take off? You're going to need plutonium. It's one of the easiest things to spot in the world, thanks to its distinctive red, spiky appearance. Hit it with your mining beam to add it to your inventory, but be careful—while your multi-tool's boltcaster and grenades will destroy the crystals, they won't give you plutonium in the process. Leave the mining to the mining beam, in this case.

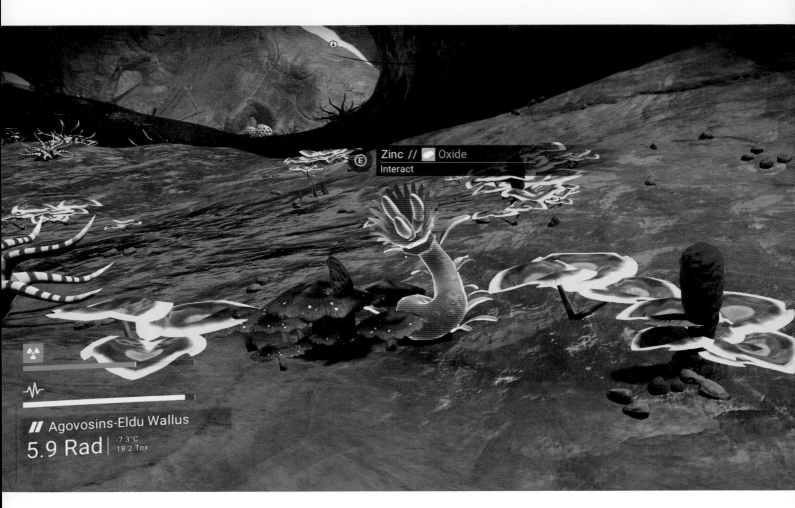

Zinc // Oxide
Interact

⚡ Agovosins-Eldu Wallus
5.9 Rad | -7.3°C 18.2 Tox

Oxides

If you want to stay alive, you're going to need to keep some oxides handy. These are used to power your suit's hazard protection and your ship's shields. They show up as a yellow icon with what appears to be a gold bar.

Iron (Common) 13.8

If you need iron, it's as close as your nearest pile of otherwise worthless rocks. Iron is incredibly common, and it's easy to fill up your inventory with piles of the stuff. Your multi-tool's grenades really shine with iron harvesting, reaping huge rewards in moments with each blast.

Zinc (Uncommon) 41.3 plants, warp cells

Zinc is tough to find in the wild, where it pops up in yellow plants. If you see one on your travels, be sure to stop by and grab it—it'll save you a few store runs later when you need it for crafting warp cells.

Titanium (Rare) 61.9 sentinels, multi-tool

Titanium is trickier to find, but sentinels are made from the stuff. Take advantage of that by starting a little trouble and disassembling the sentries that come by. It's used in a lot of multi-tool upgrades.

Platinum // △ Silicate
Interact

Agovosins-Eldu Wallus
5.9 Rad | -7.3°C
18.2 Tox

Silicates

Silicates are a component used frequently in tech upgrades for your ship and other items. They have a blue icon with a beaker on it.

Heridium (Common) 27.5

Heridium is found in building-sized deposits that are tough to miss. Like all big resource deposits, they'll be highlighted on your scanner as clusters of little squares. This is used in a ton of recipes, so keep it on hand.

Platinum (Uncommon) 55

Blue plants will give you small amounts of platinum, so, as with zinc, make sure you make an effort to collect it when you can.

Crysonite (Rare) 82.5

This looks like a blue version of plutonium. It's often grouped with plutonium, so be on the lookout for it when you spot large crystal clusters.

Neutrals

These are used in a host of crafting situations, such as your ship's warp drives and other systems. They're also a great way to make money. While neutrals can be used to create alloys (if you have the recipes) that can be sold, they're also valuable on their own. They can appear as huge deposits on planetary surfaces, or as larger asteroids while exploring space.

- Copper (Uncommon) 110

- Iridium (Uncommon) 96.3

- Nickel (Uncommon) 137.5

- Aluminum (Rare) 165

- Gold (Rare) 220

- Emeril (Rare) 275

Precious Elements

These are the rarest of the rare, so good luck finding them. One approach is to feed friendly animals—if you're lucky, they'll direct you to a source. They can also appear as strange-looking plants as you explore. Their rarity makes it tough to recommend trying to seek them out as a reliable way to make money. Your best bet is to buy them from the marketplace when you need them for a blueprint.

- Calium (Very Rare) 288.8

- Radnox (Very Rare) 302.5

- Murrine (Very Rare) 302.5

- Omegon (Very Rare) 309.4

Emeril // Neutral

Destroy

The Atlas
Your Destiny lies in the Beyond
Press M to open Galactic Map

Traintruction

Units: 91,242 ⊕

STARSHIP INVENTORY (48 SLOTS)

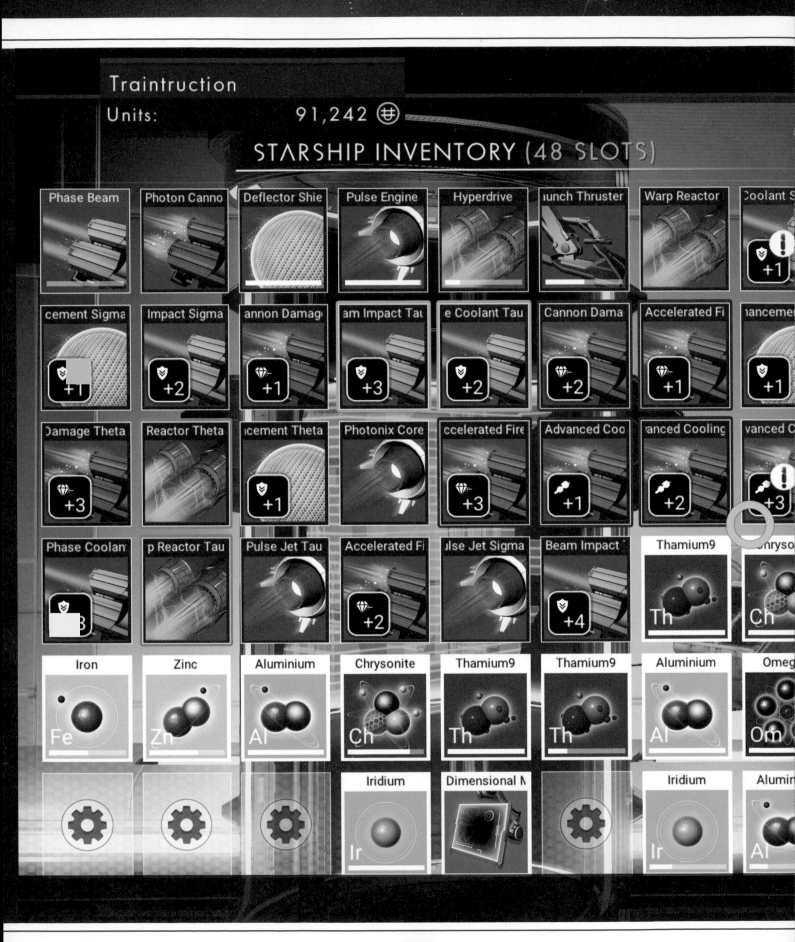

Phase Beam	Photon Canno	Deflector Shie	Pulse Engine	Hyperdrive	iunch Thruster	Warp Reactor	Coolant S +1
cement Sigma +1	Impact Sigma +2	annon Damag +1	am Impact Tau +3	e Coolant Tau +2	Cannon Dama +2	Accelerated Fi +1	iancemen +1
Damage Theta +3	Reactor Theta	icement Theta +1	Photonix Core	ccelerated Fire +3	Advanced Coo +1	anced Cooling +2	vanced C +3
Phase Coolan 3	p Reactor Tau	Pulse Jet Tau	Accelerated Fi +2	Ilse Jet Sigma	Beam Impact +4	Thamium9 Th	hrysο Ch
Iron Fe	Zinc Zn	Aluminium Al	Chrysonite Ch	Thamium9 Th	Thamium9 Th	Aluminium Al	Omeg Om
⚙	⚙	⚙	Iridium Ir	Dimensional N	⚙	Iridium Ir	Alumin Al

Ⓐ EXOSUIT | STARSHIP | MULTI-TOOL Ⓓ

Rutorisc S78
Install technology and manage your starship's cargo

WEAPONS

HEALTH

SCAN

HYPERDRIVE

RETURN Ⓟ

INTELLIGENT LIFE

There are three alien races in No Man's Sky, if you don't count all the procedurally generated beasties that are across the galaxy. Each one has its own language, culture, and overall appearance, even if your interactions with them are ultimately quite similar.

One of the biggest hurdles you'll face when trying to engage one of these aliens is not sharing a common language. You can certainly fumble your way through interactions by blindly guessing what they want, but you're better served in the long term trying to find some common ground. Information you find from knowledge stones, ruins, and monoliths can go a long way in that regard.

As you learn new words, they're incorporated into the lines of gibberish that the aliens speak. Eventually, you'll be able to use context clues to figure out what they're looking for. A damaged Korvax might sputter a bunch of nonsense, but if you see the words "rare isotope," it's likely that

he's looking for, well, a rare isotope. Give it to him instead of some carbon, and you might reap the rewards.

Here's a quick look at each of the three races, as well as some overall guidelines on how you should interact with them.

Gek

The Gek are small, reptilian, and kind of cute. Don't let that harmless exterior fool you, however. They actually have a long tradition of warfare, and they had their eyes on galactic conquest at one point in their history. Thankfully, they're now much more interested in commerce.

They're generally delighted to see you, and they're almost always ready to trade. If you don't know what they're looking for, it's safe to assume that they want cash or rare items. They're greedy, but generous, and it pays to keep these guys happy.

Korvax

The Korvax are an artificial lifeform dedicated to acquiring knowledge. Even if you don't ever see the faces behind their electronic visors, you can assume that they're probably making what amounts to a sneer. They tend to be smug and aloof.

They're keen on experimenting on you, and there are benefits to allowing them to do so in the form of rare blueprints and other valuables. Be open with information and humble, and you may walk away with some new gear. Don't expect to leave with a greater understanding of the Korvax, or anything approaching affection, however.

Vy'keen

The Vy'keen are all about bravado and honor. These large creatures have several main forms, which include a variety of facial innovations. Their mouths can include mandibles or dominant oral tentacles, but none of them prevent this race from boasting about their skills on the battlefield.

They're obsessed with multi-tools, and they'll often demand to see yours. It's a good idea to comply, and not just because they could smash you with their fists—these interactions can lead to free upgrades of your multi-tool unit. Otherwise, be brave and don't back down when you encounter these noble aliens. They'll respect you for it, even as they insist on calling you "interloper."

JOURNEY TO THE STARS

You've sped across the galaxy until your warp drive was running on fumes. You've catalogued weird creatures, some of which clearly wanted to give you a tour of their bellies. You've landed on planets that gave new meaning to the word "desolate." You know the Gek word for "syrup."

Now what?

That's the big question at the core of No Man's Sky. Exploration is the biggest part of the experience, though there is a kernel of a story to follow if you're interested. Your main goal, should you choose to accept it, is to work your way to the center of the galaxy. In the game's opening moments, the Atlas path revealed itself. You've taken the first few steps on that journey, and now it's time to walk through the rest of it.

One of the convenient things about warping through space is that you end up within an asteroid's throw of a space station. Occasionally, you'll also notice something curious when you first enter a

ARRIVE IN: 0:06
SPACE ANOMALY

214u

ARRIVE IN: 12:03
SPACE STATION

Rutorisc S78

SHIELD

Photon Ca

// Toigashiku

0.0°C | 5.0 Rad
0.0 Tox

solar system: a space anomaly. It will first make itself known on your galaxy map with "anomaly detected," but it's hard to miss this huge, metallic orb. When you see it, fly inside to begin the next leg of your journey.

The space anomaly is actually a ship that's being piloted by a couple of inquisitive aliens. Specialist Polo is a Gek, and Priest Entity Nada is a Korvax. Thanks to a strange phenomenon, you're able to understand one another perfectly. Both will help you on your journey, though in different ways.

Nada offers direct assistance, though you need to know what to ask for. He has several different options to choose from, including options that allow you to ask for resources for your journey or a shortcut to the center of the galaxy. You're certainly free to choose those, but the smart move—at least initially—is to stick to the Atlas path. You'll have plenty of time to explore those other options. When you choose the Atlas path, he'll add the location of an Atlas Interface to your galaxy map.

Polo is a little more gameplay driven. There are loads of little achievements that you'll make while playing, such as meeting certain numbers of aliens, walking various distances, or learning so many words in an alien language. Polo will give you rewards for those, so be sure to talk to him. You'll likely unlock the blueprint for the Atlas Keycard v1, which will allow you to unlock a variety of different doors in the game, including the doors on the left when you first enter a space station—doors that will lead you to stations to upgrade your suit's inventory space.

There's also a cylindrical chamber on the right side of the main chamber, which will contain a multi-tool. It may or may not be better than what you

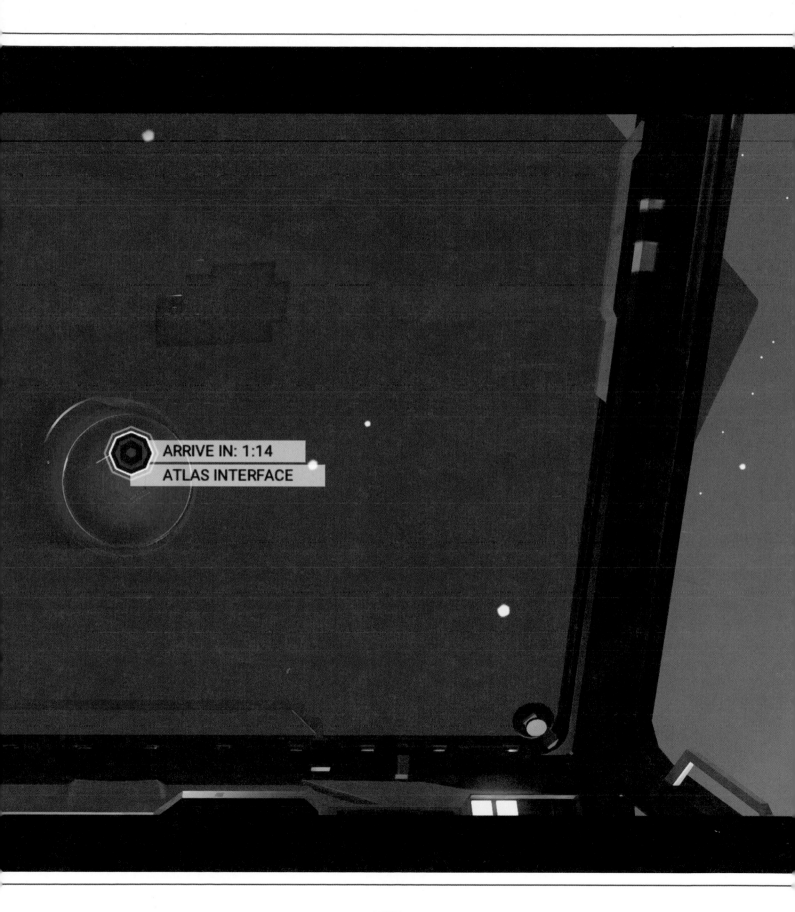

ARRIVE IN: 1:14

ATLAS INTERFACE

have currently equipped, but it's at least worth investigating. Once you have the new location on your map, it's time to bid farewell to these travelers, at least for now.

Warp to the Atlas Interface for one of the game's most impressive moments. When you arrive, you'll see another strange sight—a floating monument to your quest. Fly inside, and prepare to feel small.

When you exit your ship, you'll see the core of the Atlas Interface, which can manifest itself in several different ways. Regardless of its form, be sure that you take the time to step onto the glowing orbs of light that are arranged on the floor surrounding it. Doing so will teach you a variety of different alien words. Could this be a monument to knowledge and exploration?

After you have collected all of the orbs, approach the center of the chamber and interact with the panel in front of the object. A bit of story will play out. Choose to follow the path, and the game will present the next Atlas Interface's location to you. You'll also be given at Atlas Stone. Before you leave, be sure to collect the warp cells that are on either side of the panel.

The final leg of your structured journey will follow this loop. Move from Atlas Interface to Atlas Interface, giving in to its will and collecting the stones that it gives you. It's imperative that you keep the stones. You'll be given 10 of them total, one at each location. You can sell them, but for a fraction of the more than 2 million units it will cost to buy one back from the trade network. They take up one inventory slot each, but it's a small sacrifice to make.

When you arrive at the final Atlas Interface, you can give them your Atlas Stones in exchange for

Somuseto Atteam

Undiscovered
132,289ks

214u

Rutorisc S78

SHIELD

Photon Cannon

something. In part, this will allow you to see and interact with black holes on the galactic map—what Nada directs you toward when you choose to get a shortcut to the center of the galaxy.

Black holes will allow you to get to the center of the galaxy faster, but they will do a number on your ship. If you do choose to make use of this dazzling shortcut, expect to make repairs to your warp drive and other systems. Consider it routine maintenance for high-risk space travel.

Now that you know your ultimate destination—and, more importantly, how to get there—the rest is up to you. Some players might feel satisfied once they've finished the Atlas Path portion of the game. Others might be determined to continue on and see what exactly is at the center. The important thing to remember is that so much of the game is up to players to discover on their own.

Whether you think your trip is nearing the end or only beginning, there's one last thing that you should do. Go to the galaxy map, enter free-exploration mode, and aim toward the shining beacon that is the center of the galaxy. Move the camera toward it, keeping in mind that every single star that zips by is a solar system, with planet-sized planets teeming with life or utterly barren and hostile. Planets filled with wondrous sights and mountains of gold—or planets with atmospheres that would choke you in an instant. Keep going. With any luck, after a few minutes you'll have a bit more perspective on your place in this galaxy, fictional though it may be. No Man's Sky may put elements like mining and upgrades in the forefront, but it's really about conveying a sense of awe and wonder at the world around us, and where it is in our universe.

Don't stop exploring.

Arumnacigu YO900
Undiscovered
1,581,353ks

OTHER GAME RECOMMENDATIONS

There's nothing quite like No Man's Sky, which is why it's captured so many of our imaginations. That doesn't mean that other games don't offer their own fantastic worlds to explore. If you find yourself gravitating toward specific aspects of No Man's Sky—whether it's fighting, flying, or finding new ways to survive—we've got some recommendations for other titles that you might enjoy.

You enjoy the thrill of combat and survival in strange new worlds...

Subnautica
Developer: Unknown Worlds Entertainment
Platforms: PC, Xbox One

There's something equally alluring and frightening about the black void of the ocean depths. Subnautica capitalizes on those sensations in a survival game that challenges players to explore a mysterious undersea world, filled with secrets and threats. You're free to explore the undersea world, learning more about who—or what—came before you via strange artifacts.

This is a great game for people who are fond of No Man's Sky's undersea biomes, for obvious reasons. There's also a robust crafting element, for people who enjoy scouring an environment for resources to make new tools. And, of course, there are plenty of creatures to scan and learn about. But be careful: more than a few are protective of their habitat, and they'll protect it with tooth, claw, or whatever else is at their disposal.

Ark: Survival Evolved
Developer: Studio Wildcard, Instinct Games, Effecto Studios, Virtual Basement
Platforms: PC, PlayStation 4, Xbox One

Even in spite of your character's technological advantages, it's easy to feel naked and vulnerable in No Man's Sky. Ark: Survival Evolved takes that sensation literally. You start off without even the clothes on your back, and you're challenged with figuring out how to survive in a hostile world. To make things more complicated (and exciting), the world you're in is home to a variety of dinosaurs.

next big hunt. If that's how you've tackled No Man's Sky, theHunter: Primal sounds like the kind of game you're after. Your mission is simple: conquer a wild planet so that it can be colonized.

One again, dinosaurs are on the menu. You'll take turns hunting and being hunted by these fearsome beasts, including T. Rexes, while you look around for better weapons and other survival tools. You'll be able to take down the beasts with an arsenal that includes lowly machetes up to high-powered sniper rifles. Succeed, and you're sowing the seeds for human progress. Fail, and they might write your name on a plaque somewhere.

You're welcome to try to give it a go by yourself, but Ark encourages players to band together and work cooperatively. There's strength in numbers, after all. If you're crafty and patient enough, you can eventually tame dinosaurs. The only thing possibly cooler than getting around a planet on a spaceship might be riding around on your very own triceratops.

theHunter: Primal
Developer: Avalanche Studios
Platforms: PC

You've catalogued a wide variety of alien lifeforms on your interstellar hunt. Forget Africa's Big 5; your ship has carried you across galaxies in search of the

You're eager to explore new, uncharted places

Elite Dangerous

Developer: Frontier Developments
Platforms: PC, PlayStation 4, Xbox One

Elite Dangerous updates the classic PC game Elite in significant ways, giving players a shot at experiencing the thrill of space exploration. You're not just flying past postcard-worthy vistas, however. You'll come across hostile factions as you travel, which means you'll want to outfit your ship with the necessary arms to defend yourself.

You do that via a gameplay loop that includes mining, trading, and upgrading (or replacing) your ship. Elite Dangerous has had several expansions since its release, which have added the ability to land on planetary surfaces and even fly cooperatively with friends. If you've ever wanted to shout orders to fire on enemy spaceships and have a friend follow your command, this is a great one to try out. Frontier Developments has more expansions on the horizon, too, so expect Elite Dangerous to only get bigger.

Star Citizen

Developer: Cloud Imperium Games
Platforms: PC

Star Citizen raised more than $100 million in crowdfunding, showing that fans of space exploration are more than willing to pony up the cash for the experience. The game, designed by Wing Commander creator Chris Roberts, has an incredibly ambitious scope. Eventually, players could be able to seamlessly fly their fully modeled ship from a base, dogfight their way to a remote planet, and then land on its surface to engage in shooter-based combat. Sound familiar?

The game has a large multiplayer component, but a single-player campaign is on its way. Called Squadron-42, it features performances from high-profile actors including Mark Hamill, Gary Oldman, and more. As a work in progress, Star Citizen has its share of technical hiccups, but it's a universe worth exploring. And thanks to its regular "fly for free" promotions, you can get a taste of what it has to offer without spending a single credit.

Players can team up to create corporations, which share resources and provide protection while navigating the more treacherous areas in space. These corporations can build massive ships that have real-world value, thanks to the significant time investment spent researching and constructing the virtual vessels. Tensions can erupt in large-scale battles that feature thousands of ships fighting in real time—with the losers slinking away with losses in the tens of thousands of dollars.

You want to make new friends (or enemies) in space

Eve Online
Developer: CCP Games
Platforms: PC

The double-crosses, power plays, and internal drama that have inhabited Eve Online are enough to make Machiavelli blush with pride. The game features many elements that are seen in the space-sim genre, including a variety of customizable ships, combat, and a bustling economy. That economy is the source of much of the game's notorious intrigue.

Homeworld Remastered

Developer: Gearbox
Platforms: PC

This remaster of the classic real-time strategy game lets you explore the galaxy while milking its economy for all it's worth. The single-player campaign is a great alternative for people who want to get the sensation of lording over the opposition without involving other players. The game includes both Homeworlds 1 and 2, with updated visuals and other bells and whistles.

You manage a fleet of ships as you play, and they're persistent from mission to mission. That simple touch makes it easy to grow attached to your units, similarly to how you might feel a pang of regret when you permanently lose a powerful soldier in the XCOM games. Play your cards right, and manage your resources correctly, and you may just have a shot of returning to your titular homeworld.

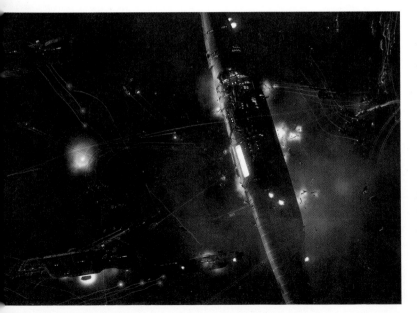

You love finding resources and building new tools to not only survive, but thrive

Minecraft

Developer: Mojang
Platforms: PC, PlayStation 4, Xbox One, Wii U, PlayStation 3, Xbox 360, Android, iOS

Minecraft makes headlines for how resourceful its players can be, who have used the game's creative tools to recreate Westeros from *Game of Thrones* or their own hometowns. As impressive as those feats can be, let's not forget that a large portion of Minecraft is built on survival.

Like No Man's Sky, Minecraft features procedurally-generated worlds, which in Minecraft's case can be created from scratch each time you start. You may find yourself in the middle of a vast desert, or in the center of a thriving village. Regardless, the world is a dangerous place and you need to outfit yourself accordingly if you hope to survive. Zombies, giant spiders, and the infamous explosive creepers could be around the next corner. Dive deep into the world to find the raw materials necessary to keep these threats at bay. Who knows? Eventually you may build your own little safe haven.

Space Engineers

Developer: Keen Software House
Platforms: PC, Xbox One

Space Engineers is a title that sums it up neatly. In the game, you're a resourceful astronaut who's able to build the ship of your dreams. You do it by harvesting minerals from asteroids and planetary surfaces by hand or via specialized mining ships. Alternately, you could hope that you stumble across the wreckage of a cargo ship or be proactive and take one down yourself. Regardless of how you get those resources, they're used to build a variety of different types of blocks, which are the necessary components for building ships or even stations.

Building these ships feels a little like working with virtual Lego, though the ability to change a block's color on the fly gives you more opportunities for customization. Just because your creation technically flies doesn't mean it will fly well; look online to see an impressive array of videos showing ships crashing spectacularly into one another. The game's physics engine accurately models inertia and velocity, which engineers should keep in mind, lest they become another statistic.

Starbound

Developer: Chucklefish Games
Platforms: PC

Starbound's pixelated, 2D presentation is similar to Terraria, but its spacefaring theme makes it a natural fit for people who enjoy No Man's Sky. Once again, your character is marooned on a distant planet after your ship crashes, and you have to explore and be resourceful to stay alive and get your ship up and running again.

The game is filled with different alien races, which you can visit once you get your ship operational again. They have their own different personalities and aesthetics, which make it a delight to explore. Will you encounter a race of penguin-like creatures? How about robots or monkeys? Work with these other lifeforms, and you can unlock special armor and other gear. If you're not feeling social, feel free to start exploring and make your own discoveries.